to Sheenagh

Shakespeare and the Psalms Mystery

Jem Bloomfield

The **Erewash Press** grew out of a group of friends who kept recommending each other obscure and unusual books. We enjoy finding old books, passing them around and talking about them.

The Press publishes e-book editions of unusual or out-of-the-way books; our main fields of interest are Christianity, theology, women's fiction and mid-century fiction, though we also range more widely. The Press has now begun to publish new works that we think would appeal to our readers and excite the same enjoyment as finding an obscure book by a favourite author, or something from your favourite genre that was out of print.

You can find out more and sign up to our mailing list at:
erewashpress.wordpress.com

Shakespeare and the Psalms Mystery
ISBN 978-1-912067-59-6
First published September 2017 by Erewash Press.

© 2017 Jem Bloomfield
Cover and typesetting © 2017 Sheenagh Bloomfield

All rights reserved. No part of this publication may be reproduced, distributed, or transmitted in any form or by any means, including photocopying, recording, or other electronic or mechanical methods, without the prior written permission of the publisher,

Acknowledgements

The formal references to other works in this book only scratch the surface of the debts I owe to friends, colleagues and previous scholars in developing the ideas expressed here. A few names in particular must stand in for the years of conversation, scholarly support and pints in pubs near libraries which gave rise to the book. Peter Kirwan is a kind and inspiring scholar, whose advice and knowledge I have benefitted from a great deal over recent years. Pascale Aebischer taught me a great deal about how academe works, and how ideas fit together. The faculty and students of the Shakespeare Institute in Stratford kindly invited me to give a couple of papers on Shakespeare and the Bible in 2016–17 whilst I was working on this book, and provided lively and thought-provoking responses. Their hospitality, intellectual and otherwise, is much appreciated. Beatrice Groves and Briony Frost were both encouraging about the project at crucial moments, and influenced its form in different ways. My thanks and love to Sheenagh for all the conversations which are in the background of this book. And thanks to Will Tosh, whose email started *Shakespeare and the Psalms Mystery* in the first place.

Contents

Prologue: A Message from the Globe	1
Arguments from History	9
The Legend and the Text	45
The Theory and the Poetry	73
Victorian Origins	111
Kipling's Daemon	153
The Story is Told…	179
The Lure of the Legend	207
Appendix: "Proofs of Holy Writ"	227

Prologue: A Message from the Globe

Last spring I received an email from Shakespeare's Globe in London. Alongside performing Shakespeare's plays in a reconstruction of a theatre from his time, they do a great deal of educational work, increasing people's appreciation of the history and context of the plays, and the world they arose from. The email was from Dr Will Tosh, a Research Fellow and Lecturer at Shakespeare's Globe, who had a peculiar question to ask: did Shakespeare help write the King James Bible? I should point out that Will had not come up with this idea himself, and in fact did not believe it was true. He had been asked by a member of the public if it was the case, and had been rather taken aback. Because of the public outreach work Will is involved with at Shakespeare's Globe, he is occasionally asked odd questions like this: people present him with myths and legends about Shakespeare and ask him to confirm or deny them. Given the unparalleled place Shakespeare holds in English-speaking culture, it is not surprising that various stories have grown up around his name.

Scholars are fond of speculating about what happened to him during the "lost years" in his life as a young man, when the historical records are frustratingly (or intriguingly) vague about where he might have been. (I was once asked by one of my own students whether Shakespeare had ever lived in her home town, a small village in the North of England, because there was a local legend that this was where the great poet had spent the lost years.) Some stories are more elaborate, such as the theories, believed by a number of people, that Shakespeare did not in fact write the plays ascribed to him, and that his name was used as a cover by another person, whether Christopher Marlowe, Francis Bacon, the Earl of Essex or Queen Elizabeth herself.

Will was used to dealing with these sort of queries, but being asked whether Shakespeare had written part of the King James Bible—specifically the 46th psalm—was a new one to him. As he explained in his message, the question was so unexpected, and the idea seemed so impossible, that his immediate instinct was to scoff at it. The idea seemed so bizarre, however, that he wondered where on earth it could have originated. He even wondered whether there was some obscure manuscript somewhere which might have given rise to this rumour, since it seemed so unlikely to have sprung from nowhere. The very impossibility of the story had made him pause. Since he knew that my research concerned the connections between Shakespeare and the Bible, and that I had just published a book on the subject, Will got in touch with me to ask if I had ever heard the rumour, and what my opinion of it was.

Before going any further, I should explain the details of the rumour itself. What I have called the "Psalm 46 legend" in this book is the idea that Shakespeare can be "found" in the 46th Psalm in the King James Bible by counting 46 words from the beginning and 46 words from the end. It states that in doing so, the reader will find the word "shake" and the word "spear". Depending on which version you hear, this may be connected to the idea that Shakespeare was 46 years old when the King James Bible was published. What this means also differs depending on the version of the legend. One variation says that the translators of the King James Bible hid Shakespeare's name in this way to show their enjoyment of his works. Another version claims that Shakespeare actually wrote this version of Psalm 46, and "signed" his work in this way. Either way, it assumes a connection between Shakespeare and Psalm 46, in a quite direct and personal way.

In fact I had heard the story before. Once years ago from an editor for whom I was reviewing crime novels, once as an odd tale from a friend of a friend (though I can't remember which friend) and once from a fellow scholar as an example of the sort of impossible thing people will believe about Shakespeare. It is one of the stranger stories that gets passed around about the man from Stratford-upon-Avon, a species of literary urban legend. Having used that term, I should state immediately that I do not believe the story. As Will thought, it simply does not make sense. For anyone reading this book simply to find out whether Shakespeare did or did not write the 46th psalm, this may be pre-empting my conclusion somewhat (though it may save them some valuable time). In my opinion, there is a wealth of historical, literary and textual evidence that he did not. Of course we can never be

100 per cent certain of almost anything in historical research: a document could turn up, or a source might reveal unforeseen implications, or a technical analysis of an artefact could suddenly throw out the careful balance of probabilities drawn from the available evidence which produces scholarly consensus. But I am reasonably confident in saying that—barring a personal letter turning up from Ben Jonson asking William Shakespeare how he's getting along with that psalm they asked him to write—this rumour is untrue.

That does not mean, however, that the matter ends there. On the contrary, for me it was where the story began. I wrote back to Dr Tosh, explaining that I knew of the story, and agreeing with him that it could not be true. In order to give some more authority to this statement than my personal "Nah, no chance", I made a quick survey of the relevant sources. I consulted some 16th-century Bible translations, the biographies of a pair of bishops, confirmed the font used in the King James Bible, searched another poet's version of the Psalms. After that I was in a position to write a fuller response to the enquiry from Shakespeare's Globe, giving some solid historical and literary justification for my opinion. That was not the only reason I'd delved into the historical sources, though. The Psalm 46 rumour had always interested me, partly because it was so bizarre, and I enjoyed tracing the various ways in which it could have possibly been true, and marshalling the evidence to prove it was not. The story branched off into questions about the translation of the King James Bible, the theatre industry of Shakespeare's time, the religious politics of England under James I, the way Early Modern books were printed, and attitudes to the Bible. Though I did not think the story was true, proving it untrue opened up much more interesting issues.

One of the most interesting issues it raised was that of the legend itself. Why did anyone believe it in the first place? Who had the idea? Why might it have suggested itself to them? What did people find attractive about this rumour, and why did they repeat it to others? Why, for example, was it repeated in a respectable commentary on the Psalms published by a major US Christian publisher in 2014? Answering those questions involved investigating a whole other set of issues: the world of Edwardian literary culture, the temple worship of Ancient Israel, the reputation of the Bible in universities, and the sermons of modern pastors. Hovering over all of them were the bigger questions of how Shakespeare became the most famous author in the history of the English language, and how the Bible has been treated differently over the last few hundred years. From a single question about the authorship of a psalm in the King James Bible, I found myself chasing down the passages of historical research in a dozen different directions. This book is the result of that headlong chase, and tells some of the stories I came across along the way. As I said above, I do not think Shakespeare wrote the 46th psalm. That might be disappointing to some readers: it would have been a weird and cool anecdote if it had been true. But like anyone who deals with the literary past, I think the real story is far more fascinating and surprising than any urban legend. This book's title reflects that idea: the real mysteries around Shakespeare and the Bible are not this peculiar legend, but the deep and engrossing history of these texts, the centuries of human emotion, reflection and hope bound up with them. The legend of Psalm 46 claims to tell us a secret, but it directs our attention away from the deeper and more rewarding mysteries.

Arguments from History

The first way I would like to explore the Psalm 46 legend is through the histories of the works of Shakespeare and the King James Bible. Setting them in a historical context immediately casts doubt on the legend's truth, and the more their historical background is explored, the less plausible it seems. In short, much modern culture tends to regard the King James Bible and the *Collected Works* of Shakespeare as two enormously imposing volumes from the same historical era. They have had vast influence on the literature, culture, language and religion of the subsequent centuries, and, looking back, many people would regard them as the pinnacles of English-speaking culture from that period. Part of the impetus to find a connection between Shakespeare and the Bible, I suspect, comes from this sense that they are the two greatest achievements of British culture, and they were created at around the same time within quite a small country. It makes intuitive sense that there would be some overlap. Like David Scott's Victorian painting, "Queen Elizabeth Viewing the Performance of *The Merry Wives of Windsor* at the Globe Theatre", which depicts an incident which never happened, the legend looks back to Early Modern England and suggests that these two incredible literary events must have had some influence on each other. Shakespeare and the King James Bible simply feel as if they belong together somehow. However, this was not the case in the period when they first appeared. As this chapter will show, contemporaries would have found the idea of a connection between Shakespeare's plays and the King James Bible very curious, and a historically-informed reading of the legend makes it seem increasingly implausible.

Shakespeare's theatre in Shakespeare's time

This historical difference between Shakespeare's lifetime and our own era is particularly striking when we consider the theatre. Though modern English-speaking theatre is deeply influenced by Shakespeare's work, and being able to perform and direct Shakespeare is often used as the mark of a "proper" theatre artist with a suitable mastery of their craft, our sense of what theatre itself means is very different from that of the people of

Shakespeare's time. For modern culture, theatre represents high culture. It is relatively expensive, certainly when compared to more "low-brow" options, such as Netflix, DVDs or karaoke, providing a barrier to immediate or casual participation. The customs which surround theatre attendance also tend to increase the cost, including slightly more formal dress than other leisure activities and accessories such as programmes. Though these may not be intended to exclude people, they hedge theatre about with the trappings of a special occasion. It takes place in imposing buildings, saturated with decades (and even centuries) of history, and often containing the pictures of notable actors from previous generations, which increases the sense of a self-conscious cultural inheritance. Theatre craft is part of a tradition of elite art, a complex and (to some people) rather old-fashioned cultural past-time with intricate rules and requiring a high level of education in both its creators and its audiences. Whether old-fashioned or not, it carries great cachet: attending the theatre is one of the activities which sociologists identify as producing "cultural capital", giving people who regularly attend it an air of social importance and good judgement. These are not simply free-floating markers of artistic taste, or abstract preferences in entertainment, but work as markers of real differences in people's life chances and perceived place in society. An investigation into the economic and social structure of Britain in 2013 found that people earning over £200,000 a year were significantly more likely than other groups to own extremely valuable house property, know a member of the aristocracy personally, and attend the theatre regularly.[1]

That combination of social rank and theatre experience appears in another sense in Britain, as the most famous and successful theatre actors are often granted a knighthood or damehood by the royal family. This is one of the highest awards within the honours system, and actors can join the line of "knights and dames of the theatre" who have received the same accolade in previous centuries, gaining an association with the past which legitimates present social distinctions. The royal family are not the only powerful supporters of the theatre as an art form and an institution: traditional theatre is expensive to stage as well as to attend, and many nations subsidise their theatres heavily, spending millions upon millions of their citizens' money to ensure that theatre continues to flourish. Along with this support from the state often comes a duty placed on the theatres to make their performances as widely available as possible, and they may discount tickets, put on special shows for schools and colleges, host community arts groups and invest time and money in "outreach" to groups in their society which do not usually attend the theatre or benefit from the cultural capital it can provide.

In short, theatre is a serious matter in modern culture. It is regarded by almost everyone as an elite activity, and one which confers cultural, intellectual and social benefits upon the people who take part in it. Theatre is somehow felt to be good for people, on both a personal level (seen in the efforts spent on getting young people from disadvantaged backgrounds to participate in theatre, or the money spent by better-off parents in taking their children to see Shakespeare) and on a communal level (seen in the subsidies provided by governments to theatres to make sure they continue to be part of the national cultural life). This is more or less the opposite of the way theatres were regarded in Shakespeare's England. In the late 16th and early 17th century, theatres were wildly popular and regarded as something of a menace by many of those in power. The big outdoor theatre buildings themselves, like the Globe, were dirty, smelly and packed with audiences who had mostly not paid very much to attend. These audiences' behaviour was not at all the respectful and appreciative silence to be found in theatres today: they apparently chatted, gambled, bought food and drink and generally had a lively time of it whilst the actors were performing in front of them. Contrary to popular myth, they did not throw fruit and vegetables, whether rotten or fresh. Actors were at least spared the indignity of wiping insalubrious tomatoes off their faces whilst trying to tackle a soliloquy. But the audience were certainly not particularly anxious about the feelings or the artistry of those on stage: they had come to a popular entertainment venue, not a palace of elite culture. (The smaller private playhouses attracted a more socially elevated clientele, who were more conscious of attending an artistic performance, though even here we do not find a sense that theatre is morally improving or socially beneficial.) Theatres in Early Modern London are often discussed alongside the other kinds of entertainment available to theatre-goers at an equivalent price and venue, giving an idea of the social and cultural space they occupied in the city, and in the minds of those attending. Where for modern theatres, the equivalent alternatives might be a performance of a symphony in a concert hall, or an exhibition of paintings in an art museum, a couple of the most likely other options for Shakespeare's audiences were bear-baitings and public executions. Watching animals fight each other for sport, or forming part of the crowd as a criminal was publicly subjected to capital punishment, appear to have been the forms of entertainment jostling theatrical plays for the attention of their potential visitors. It is a rather different image to the consciously artistic world of the theatre today.

As might be expected, given the picture of Early Modern theatres I have been sketching, the authorities were not especially keen to see this activity become a major part of their national life. It is true that the theatre companies enjoyed the patronage of aristocrats: due to the draconian laws about unemployment, actors had to be technically the servants of a noble figure, and so the companies had names such as The Earl of Derby's Men, or The Admiral's Men. The theatre company Shakespeare belonged to even moved from being The Lord Chamberlain's Men to being The King's Men, when they attracted the attention and appreciation of James I. However, the enjoyment of theatre as entertainment by socially elite figures did not make the actors themselves respectable, not did it mean that everyone in authority wanted theatres to thrive. In fact, the City Fathers in London did everything they could to make running a theatre as difficult as possible. They banned theatres from being built within the parts of London under their legal jurisdiction, meaning that the companies could only erect buildings around the edges of the city, in the same areas where brothels and other socially disreputable establishments clustered. Whilst modern corporations often display their enlightened taste and good citizenship by sponsoring theatre productions or contributing to fundraising appeals, the business interests of Shakespeare's time were decidedly against the theatre. They complained that their workers, particularly the young apprentices, neglected their work and snuck off to the theatre instead of industriously plying their trades as they ought. The religious authorities were similarly keen to suppress the theatre, and numerous sermons, tracts and letters from churchmen rail against acting and theatre-going. One particular area of concern for them was that, since no women could perform on the Early Modern stage, the female characters were played by young men in dresses and make-up. This sort of gender subversion was morally disgraceful to the religious leaders of the time, and they declared it could lead to the breakdown of the God-given order, as the lines between men and women became blurred, and men found each other "unnaturally" attractive. Some churchmen, particularly those within the Puritan movement, also believed that the plagues which appeared from time to time in Shakespeare's London were judgements visited by God on the city for its irreligious ways, and its toleration of theatres.[2] Overall, theatres and their activities were not held in particularly high esteem in Early Modern England. They were popular, but (despite this or because of it) they did not have the cultural cachet we associate with their modern equivalents, and they were explicitly disapproved of by the religious and civic authorities. It would certainly seem surprising to anyone in the 17th century that theatres might be regarded as good for people, or contributing to the moral and social life of the nation.

The purpose of outlining the differences between modern theatres and the theatres of Shakespeare's time, and their dramatically contrasting places in culture, is to show how likely this makes it that Shakespeare's name would be hidden in the King James Bible. Whilst for modern readers Shakespeare and the Bible have an apparently natural association, given their cultural authority and artistic value, there would have been no such obvious connection for people at the time. A writer who turned out entertaining pieces for the public playhouses is not the sort of person they would associate with the Bible sanctioned by King James. Playwrights were not particularly significant people in the national culture. Indeed, many people who attended the theatres would not have known who wrote the plays being performed in front of them. Just as modern cinema-goers do not usually rush to see a film because they are fans of the scriptwriter or the director of photography (unless they are serious cinephiles), many of the audiences at Early Modern theatres did not care about who had provided the words for the show. Again, there is evidence that the spectators at the smaller, and more elite, indoor playhouses (where Shakespeare's works were also performed) knew the names of the playwrights, and liked to compare their artistic styles, but this would have been less usual at the big open-air theatres like the Globe. One striking fact when considering Shakespeare's fame (or lack of it) is the absence of his name from the early printings of his plays. When *Romeo and Juliet* was first printed in the 1590s, it was issued in the cheap flimsy format known as a "quarto", and did not have Shakespeare's name anywhere on it. The same is true of *Richard III* and the first *Henry VI* plays, which we now regard as major artistic achievements and central parts of Shakespeare's claim to literary and theatrical greatness. To the book-buying public of the 1590s, these were popular stage shows which were printed under the name of the theatre company so audiences could read the text of the performances they had enjoyed. These were not the

"Works of Shakespeare", but more akin to tie-in products of the theatre industry. By the time the King James Bible was produced in the 1610s, Shakespeare's name was much better known, and some printers had even taken to putting his name on plays which he had not written, to attract interest from readers. Nonetheless, this meant he was famous for being part of an entertainment industry, which was far from respectable, and certainly at the other extreme of English culture from the scholarly and devout undertakings of the Bible translators.

The translation and the translators

I'd now like to turn to those translators, and discuss the way the King James Bible emerged in the early 17th century. As with the account of the theatres above, I think this sheds light on the plausibility of the legend, and will also explain the kinds of textual analysis I'll be undertaking in the next chapter. Like the *Collected Works* of Shakespeare, the King James Bible tends to look rather monumental and inevitable in hindsight, looming up out of the mists of history as a landmark which we can use to navigate the centuries around it. To people at the time, though, the translation was not so obviously a defining moment for religion and literature, and examining its history provides an alternative perspective on the book.

In practical terms, the King James Bible was a side-effect of the religious politics of Early Modern Europe. The various religious, social and political upheavals which we group together as "the Reformation" had left Europe with ongoing tensions and conflicts. These can be seen in geographical terms by comparing the religious allegiances of different nations at a particular moment: for example, when Elizabeth I was on the throne, England was a largely Protestant state, and Spain an extremely Catholic one, and the religious strife was interwoven with military and political rivalries which broke out into open war at moments such as the attempted invasion by the Spanish Armada. It can also be looked at across time, by tracing the changes within a single nation: England provides another good example, being officially Catholic and then Protestant after the break with Rome under Henry VIII, more thoroughly Protestant and reforming under the young Edward VI, returning to Catholicism under Queen Mary and Protestant again under Elizabeth I. As Mary's nickname "Bloody Mary" suggests, these changes in official religious policy involved widespread violence and the suppression of groups who disagreed with the monarch's beliefs; whole countries did not simply "change" their religious beliefs along with the official line. They were also subject to influence and threat from beyond national borders: the Spanish Armada mentioned above is an obvious example, as is the declaration by the Pope that it would be allowable (and even meritorious) for Catholic English people to assassinate Queen Elizabeth. The later plot to blow up the Houses of Parliament, which led to the arrest of Guy Fawkes (a date still commemorated in Britain today) was an attempt by Catholic noblemen to destroy James I and his government in order to restore a Catholic monarchy. Religion was a major part of the political and cultural strife in Early Modern Europe, both between nations and within them, and the most obvious distinction was between Protestants and Catholics.

When James I came to the throne of England in 1603, one of his particular ambitions was to heal the religious divisions within Britain and even across Europe. He had already been King of Scotland for some years, and experienced the difficulties of religious politics, and he hoped for a more peaceful Europe. Elizabeth I's religious policy had stressed her desire to accommodate a range of religious views (within narrow limits) under Protestant rule, and the phrase "via media", or "middle way between two extremes" is often used to describe her attitude. (This did not stop her from executing significant numbers of her subjects, and suppressing the activities of groups which went too far in either the Catholic or Protestant direction: Early Modern notions of religious tolerance were much more limited than later ideas.) James wanted to carry this notion even further, and saw himself as a religious peacemaker, seeking alliances with other nations and even attempting to marry one of his sons to the King of Spain's daughter. At home, James—who also regarded himself as an intellectual—called a conference at Hampton Court which he hoped would go some way to solve the religious disputes within Britain.

The conference was sparked by a petition sent by Puritan ministers at the very beginning of James' reign, to forestall the sympathy towards Catholics which the Puritans worried would be evident in the new king's policies. It was referred to as the Millenary Petition, due to the story that it was signed by a thousand ministers (which historians cannot corroborate). Dealing with these religious divisions head-on, James summoned major figures from both the more Protestant and more Catholic movements and held three days of meetings at Hampton Court with himself as the chairman and adjudicator. Though I have been referring to "Protestants" and "Catholics" in broad terms, as if they were entirely separate groups, these religious views and identities existed along a spectrum. It was illegal for Roman Catholic priests to carry on their ministry within England (though some did and died for their faith), and it was illegal for Protestants to set up churches in defiance of the national Church of England. Between those two extremes were ministers within the established church who held to the Reformed faith or the Catholic tradition to greater or lesser extents. The "sides" of the Hampton Court Conference represented these contrasting parties within the Church of England, though the Puritan group was made up of moderate rather than extreme members of their movement. Amongst the issues at debate during the conference was the government of the Church of England, the number and meaning of the sacraments, and the training and provision of ministers. The suggestion for a new translation of the Bible arose almost as an accident, due to discussions over the wording of passages in the Scriptures, but it appealed to James, and he commissioned a new version.

Orders and Instructions

The translators of the King James Bible were issued with a series of principles which would guide the project, and ensure that the relatively large number of people involved had a sense of its overall purpose, as well as supplying some answers to ecclesiastical FAQs on particular issues. In practice, we cannot know how far these instructions represented the wishes of the people who instigated the translation, and how scrupulously they were followed in the process of translation, but it does provide some insight into the declared parameters of the work.[3] They are worth quoting at length, both to show the way the translation was being imagined before it even existed, and to show the problems or controversies which were involved in its production:

1. The ordinary Bible read in the church, commonly called the Bishops' Bible, to be followed, and as little altered as the truth of the original will permit.

2. The names of the prophets, and the holy writers, with the other names of the text, to be retained, as nigh as may be, according as they are vulgarly used.

3. The old ecclesiastical words to be kept, viz. the word "church" not to be translated "congregations" etc.

4. When a word hath diverse significations, that to be kept which hath been most commonly used of the ancient fathers, being agreeable to the propriety of the place, and the analogy of the faith.

5. The division of the chapters to be altered, either not at all, or as little as may be, if necessity so require.

6. No marginal notes at all to be affixed, but only for the explanation of the Hebrew or Greek words which cannot, without some circumlocution, so briefly and fitly be expressed in the text.

7. Such quotations of places to be marginally set down as shall serve for the fit reference of one scripture to another.

8. Every particular man of each company to take the same chapter or chapters, and having translated or amended them severally by himself, where he thinketh good, all to meet together, confer what they have done, and agree for their parts what shall stand.

9. As any one company hath dispatched any one book in this manner, they shall send it to the rest, to be considered of seriously and judiciously, for His Majesty is very careful in this point.

10. If any company, upon the review of the book so sent, doubt or differ upon any place, to send them word thereof, to note the place and withal send their reasons, to which if they consent not, the difference to be compounded at the general meeting, which is to be of the chief persons of each company, at the end of the work.

11. When any place of special obscurity is doubted of, letters to be directed, by authority, to send to any learned man in the land for his judgement of such a place.

12. Letters to be sent from every bishop to the rest of his clergy, admonishing them of this translation in hand, and to move and charge as many as being skilful in the tongues; and having taken pains in that kind, to send his particular observations to the company, either at Westminster, Cambridge or Oxford.

13. The directors in each company to be the deans of Westminster and Chester for that place, and the King's professors in Hebrew and Greek in each university.

14. These translations to be used when they agree better with the text than the Bishops' Bible: Tyndale's, Matthew's, Coverdale's, Whitchurch's, Geneva.

15. Besides the said directors mentioned, three or four of the most ancient and grave divines, in either of the universities, not employed in translating, to be assigned to the Vice-Chancellor, upon conference with the rest of the heads, to be overseers of the translations as well Hebrew as Greek, for the better observation of the 4th rule above specified.

These might not be the instructions we might have expected to be issued to the translators of the King James Bible, given the way the book is discussed in modern culture. There is nothing here explicitly about theology, good English or poetic power, the aspects for which the book is mostly valued today. They are mostly concerned with procedure and with textual details. A 21st-century reader might be forgiven for finding them somewhat lacking in grandeur. This does not mean they are not revealing, however. The assumptions they make, the points which they seem to assume everyone involved already understands, are even more telling than what they consciously articulate. Several ideas seem to underpin these instructions which are relevant to my investigation of the Psalm 46 legend. Firstly, this is a profoundly conservative document (using that term in the everyday sense, rather than politically or theologically). The very first principle specifies the text upon which the King James Bible should be based, and instructs the translators to vary as little from it as possible. It is taken for granted that the rewriting of the Bible will not involve an entirely new set of words, but will be an adjustment and correction of an existing

English version. The 14th principle picks up strongly on this assumption, even providing the translators with a list of other English Bibles which they can use to supply a different version of a line (or word within the line) if they think the Bishops' Bible doesn't quite get it right. Before simply replacing a word or rephrasing a line, the instructions assume that they will want to compare the Bishops' version with the others, and—if possible—use an already existing translation, even from a version with which they might disagree in its overall political or theological emphasis. Admittedly it doesn't suggest the Catholic Douai-Rheims translation as an option, but it does include the Geneva and Tyndale versions, both of which James had serious problems with on political and ecclesiological grounds.

Mentioning politics highlights the second emphasis which underpins the project: it is a political project in both its linguistic methods and its personnel management. The third instruction that "The old ecclesiastical words to be kept" shows its intentions fairly clearly, even before the specific example "viz. the word 'church' not to be translated 'congregations' etc."

Part of James' issue with some previous translations was their undermining of established religious order by translating the accounts of the early church in ways which did not use the accepted terminology of the Church of England and the Church of Scotland. For example, "congregation" rather than "church" presented an image of people gathering together as a group to worship and share the Christian life, rather than an institution or a building; this was the vision of Christianity which Dissenting groups like the Presbyterians took. Likewise "presbyter" rather than priest, and "overseer" rather than "bishop", which both redescribed these people in ways which stressed their activities and roles rather than their place in a hierarchy or their distinct status as clergy. More generally, using different words for these terms suggested there was a gap between the world of the New Testament and the church as it officially existed in Britain: if there were no "priests" or "bishops" in the world of Acts or the churches Paul visited, then the people who currently called themselves by these titles were not the equivalents of the apostles and their followers. James was very suspicious of any such tendency, and linked it directly to his own authority, having said pithily at another time "no bishop, no king". The 13th principle also reminds us of the political nature of the project, with the overseers of the translations being identified as the "King's professors". These were positions at the universities filled by people specifically nominated by the Crown, and thus particularly loyal to the King's interests and point of view. The third assumption which emerges from the instructions is who will be involved in the process: the document imagines the translators potentially consulting whomever they think will be erudite enough to solve a specific problem (point 11), and the bishops searching their areas for people who could contribute their expertise (point 12), but the pool of people who might fit into these categories is quite small. It never specifies that only scholars and priests (and priests who are scholars) are to be involved in the translation, but this is surely because the instructions assume that goes without saying. It is part of the underlying assumptions of this project that a very limited range of people will be suitable. Finally, the instructions imagine a highly collaborative way of working on the text. The translators are to work through all the books which have been assigned to their "company" on their own before meeting up with the others to compare what they have done (point 8), when they have done that they produce an agreed text and should send this version to the other companies (point 9), and allow any objections to be raised or alterations to be suggested (point 10). This might sound an extremely haphazard way to start, since the individual translators might come up with very different translations and have to waste a lot of time in producing a common version, but (as we have seen) they were not translating freestyle from the original texts. Rather, they were marking up adjustments and amendments from the Bishops' Bible, and considering which of the other English versions specified might supply any required changes before venturing their own word or phrase. In practice, the process seems to have been less rigorously collaborative between companies, but the project is assumed to be based on team work, group discussion and scholarly consensus.

I have picked out these tendencies in the instructions given to the translators, and the assumptions which underlie them, for two reasons. They are the aspects which might seem unexpected to a modern reader, and thus can help us understand the mental world of the translators better. As I have been suggesting, part of what clouds our thinking about Shakespeare and the King James Bible is the accumulated ideas about these books when they are seen from the early 21st century: they look very different when viewed through the evidence we possess from the early 17th century. Most of these tendencies are also strong arguments against the likelihood of the Psalm 46 legend being true. The emphasis on the use of a previous translation (the Bishops' Bible), and the selection of other translations to be used in correcting or patching lines which need alteration, cuts down the freedom which the people working on the translation had to put whatever words they wished into a particular line. If Shakespeare wrote Psalm 46, his work involved choosing from a very narrow range of possible words, whilst altering a text that already existed. If the translators decided to hide the playwright's name in the text, they were similarly restricted in their ability to put words in on a whim. The collaborative nature of the project also provides problems for the Psalm 46 legend. No individual translator was responsible for the exact wording of any particular line within a psalm, let alone a whole psalm. If they did decide to hide the words in particular positions, they could not be certain that the word would stay in that position without revision, and they presumably needed to be prepared to argue in rigorous textual and linguistic terms for why that alteration needed to happen, and why it had to be in that particular form. The alternative—that the entire company of translators working on the Psalms decided to hatch a plan all together to hide Shakespeare's name—seems even more improbable. It is unlikely that they would all be enthusiastic about the work of a particular poet and dramatist, at least to the extent of rearranging their serious task by hiding his name inside Psalm 46. Even if they did, they would have to be prepared for another company to notice the alteration they had made, and object to it on textual grounds, leaving the Psalms company in the position of defending their joint prank without explaining it. Given some of the people involved in the translation of the King James Bible, the chances of a consensus developing around how witty it would be to hide a playwright's name in the text are extremely small. For example, one of the instigators of the project was John Rainolds, who had a dramatic and controversial relationship with the theatre of his time.[4] Rainolds was the leader of the Puritan party who attended the Hampton Court conference, and was outspoken in his criticism of elements like the sign of the cross and the use of vestments and incense which seemed to him (and other Puritans) to demonstrate a damaging concern with the outward show of religious worship. It was no coincidence that the Puritans, who preferred plain services without the elaborate ritual elements of their more Catholic colleagues in the English church, were also implacably opposed to the theatre and to anyone involved in putting on plays. In fact Rainolds had not always been a Puritan: his family's religious views were split, and he only became convinced of the truth of the Puritan position during his time as a student at Oxford. In his earlier years, Rainolds had even performed in a play in honour of Queen

Elizabeth's visit to the city, receiving a reward from the queen for his portrayal of Hippolyta in Richard Edward's *Palaemon and Arcyte*. However, Rainolds' opinions towards the theatre changed in line with his religious leanings, and no Puritan of the early 17th century would have approved of stage plays. We have specific evidence of this in Rainolds' case, since in 1592 he was invited to attend some plays at Christ Church College, and when his intended host (Thomas Thornton) wouldn't take no for an answer, Rainolds wrote an extensive letter explaining his reasons for disapproving of all theatrical performance. Apparently hearing of this document, the writer of the plays in question (William Gager) added an extra epilogue to the end of one of the works, in which Momus (the Greek god of carping criticism) appears to give a speech attacking theatre, and is roundly rebuked and proved wrong within the play. Gager then published the extra scenes in another of his books, and had a copy of the volume provocatively delivered to Rainolds himself. The two men then engaged in a series of letters debating the legitimacy of theatre and plays (with a law professor being drawn into the dispute on Gager's side), and in 1599 the letters were published by a Puritan printing press under the title of *The Overthrow of Stage Plays*. Rainolds' particular objections to drama included the claims that actors had always been held in contempt by respectable people since Classical times, that plays encouraged people to profane the Sabbath day, and that men dressing in women's clothes directly contravened the laws laid down in Deuteronomy. However successful the teenaged Rainolds had been playing the female role of Hippolyta onstage, he was entirely in opposition to the theatre as an older man. It is worth noting that the performances he objected to in this case were not even the shows put on at the public playhouses, but a set of private plays for invited guests in an academic setting at Oxford. If he could not countenance being present at this refined and erudite gathering, he would have regarded the rowdy and rambunctious public theatres like the Globe with horror. Rainolds was not specifically involved in the translation of the Psalms, but the group which was assigned them included another churchman with strongly Puritan tendencies, Laurence Chaderton.[5] Another ex-Catholic who radically changed his religious views at university, Chaderton had been one of Rainolds' party at the Hampton Court conference, and when he was the head of Emmanuel College in Cambridge he ran it on strictly Protestant principles, with plain clothing worn during services, and the communion cup being passed around the seated men to avoid any suggestion of "Popish" ritual by kneeling. After the conference Chaderton became something of a figurehead for the more Puritan clergy of the Church of England; given this, and his identification with Rainolds' group, it seems unbelievable that he would have a taste for the commercial theatre. Beyond the questions of personal taste and preference, the writings of clergymen of the period show how far apart the spheres of the church and the theatre were felt to be. Even when not specifically attacking or criticising actors or playhouses, the religious works of the 16th and 17th century often take it for granted that the theatre should be despised. For example, in *The Reformed Pastor*, the minister Richard Baxter advises clergy that they should maintain a moral life as an example to their congregations, remarking at one point:

> They will give you leave to preach against their sins, and to talk as much as you will for godliness in the pulpit, if you will let them alone afterwards, and be friendly and merry with them when you have done, and talk as they do, and live as they, and be indifferent with them in your conversation. For they take the pulpit to be but a stage; a place where preachers must show themselves, and play their parts; where you have liberty for an hour to say what you list; and what you say they regard not, if you show them not, by saying it personally to their faces, that you were in good earnest, and did indeed mean them.[6]

Baxter is so certain that his readers will understand that "a stage" here represents insincerity, meaninglessness and deception that he does not need to spell the points out. The implications of the term are clear enough that he can use it to criticise some other preachers. There is also a strong impression here that associating theatre with the church is degrading to the latter, and that they should be kept apart. A similar idea appears in Bishop John Jewel's *The Apology of the Church of England*. "Apology" here does not carry its modern sense of contrition and repentance, but rather an intellectual defence of something: Jewel's book is a justification of the Church of England against criticisms, and contains a significant portion of polemic against Roman Catholicism and the claims of the Pope. During these rhetorical attacks, he declares that:

> And we justly blame the bishops of Rome, who, without the word of God, without the authority of the holy fathers, without any example of antiquity, after a new guise, do not only set before the people the sacramental bread to be worshipped as God, but do also carry the same about upon an ambling horse, whithersoever themselves journey, as in old times the Persians' fire and the relics of the goddess Isis, were solemnly carried about in procession: and have brought the sacraments of Christ to be used now as a stage play and a solemn sight: to the end, that men's eyes should be fed with nothing else but with mad gazings and foolish gauds.[7]

The stream of criticism here moves from suggesting that Roman Catholic practice disregards the authorities of the Church, to the idea that it is similar to ancient pagan worship, to a comparison with the theatre. The stage is not in good company here, to put it mildly. As in *The Reformed Pastor*, theatre appears in this passage as something so self-evidently different from (and unworthy of) religion that simply by saying that Roman Catholics "have brought the sacraments of Christ to be used now as a stage play" Jewel can condemn them in strong terms. Certainly individual churchmen might have liked dramatic literature, or taken a milder line on university drama than Rainolds, or thought that the theatre was enjoyable in its own way, but the general public discourse around the two subjects assumed that the Church and there theatre were entirely antithetical, and should never be combined.

Beside the question of whether Chaderton, or any other strict clergyman of the time, might have had a secret fondness for the disreputable drama of the public playhouses, it is worth considering what would be involved in hiding Shakespeare's name inside the psalms, as the legend suggests happened. I have already mentioned the formidable technical, practical and organisational difficulties with such a scheme, which would need to involve agreement amongst a group of churchmen, who then carried it out knowing that their placement of the words might be queried by someone else further down the line. Perhaps even more serious (though more subjective) are the moral and ideological implications of the Second Cambridge Company engineering the words' order. Given the seriousness of the task the translators had been set, and their belief that they were handling the word of God, it is difficult to imagine them deliberately changing the order of the words for a cheap joke. The instructions to the companies which I quoted above show the gravity with which particular words were treated, and how carefully the translators were expected to be scrutinising every phrase of the text. Though this is an admittedly subjective judgement, I can't read the documents and sources surrounding the production of the King James Bible, and believe that these people would switch the words around for a frivolous purpose. Even the limited extent to which we can enter into their mindset from 400 years later makes it just feel wrong. However, I only offer this subjective judgement after a great deal of more objective evidence and historical context, which I think is more persuasive than my conviction of what "feels wrong". In the next chapter, I will examine the claims of the Psalm 46 legend from a textual point of view, scrutinising the text of the psalm itself and exploring the texts which preceded it. This investigation will range across the King James Bible, the hidden patterns in the Hebrew Bible and some very rude jokes in Shakespeare's sonnets; and as with this chapter, I think the real stories are much more absorbing than the legend we are discussing.

The Legend and the Text

In the previous chapter I explored the historical situations of Shakespeare's theatre and the translation of the King James Bible, setting the Psalm 46 legend in context to provide a better sense of its probability. I would now like to turn to the text of the psalm itself, and investigate it in more detail. Since the legend's plausibility depends on small textual details, scrutinising the words of the text (including their order and their origin) can shed light on the likelihood that it is true. In this chapter I shall argue that the history of the psalm as it appears in the King James Bible strongly weighs against the legend, since it was based on existing English versions and was not invented in this particular form for the new Bible. There are indeed "secret patterns" and words hidden in the psalms, as I will show, but these are part of a much older tradition of Hebrew poetry and are bound up with the devotional history of the texts, not the popularity of an English playwright at the turn of the 17th century. I will examine both these verbal patterns, and the way that Shakespeare "hid" his own name in his sonnets, in order to show that the words supposedly hidden in the psalm do not work in the same way. As with the historical investigation, this chapter suggests that the Psalm 46 legend in fact offers a rather simplified and prosaic view of Shakespeare and the King James Bible; whilst purporting to give insight into a mystery it obscures the complexities and mysteries which are embodied in these texts.

Forty-six and Forty-seven: Testing the Legend

The Psalm 46 legend, as I mentioned in the introduction, is based on the idea that anyone counting 46 words from the beginning and 46 words from the end will find the words "shake" and "spear". From this observation, people have constructed stories such as Shakespeare being paid to write this version of the psalm, or the translators being fans of his work and hiding a joke in the text: but it begins from this observation about the positions of the words. It is worth reproducing the psalm in full, as it appears in the King James Bible, with the words highlighted:

1. God is our refuge and strength, a very present help in trouble.
2. Therefore will not we fear, though the earth be removed, and though the mountains be carried into the midst of the sea;
3. Though the waters thereof roar and be troubled, though the mountains **shake** with the swelling thereof. Selah.
4. There is a river, the streams whereof shall make glad the city of God, the holy place of the tabernacles of the most High.
5. God is in the midst of her; she shall not be moved: God shall help her, and that right early.
6. The heathen raged, the kingdoms were moved: he uttered his voice, the earth melted.
7. The LORD of hosts is with us; the God of Jacob is our refuge. Selah.
8. Come, behold the works of the LORD, what desolations he hath made in the earth.
9. He maketh wars to cease unto the end of the earth; he breaketh the bow, and cutteth the **spear** in sunder; he burneth the chariot in the fire.
10. Be still, and know that I am God: I will be exalted among the heathen, I will be exalted in the earth.
11. The LORD of hosts is with us; the God of Jacob is our refuge. Selah.

The first textual problem with the legend will be obvious to anyone who did the boring work of counting the words in the psalm above: "spear" is not the 46th word from the end of the psalm. In fact, "in" is the 46th, a far less exciting word, and "spear" is the

47th. The only way to make "spear" the 46th word, and fit the legend, is to ignore the last word of the psalm, which is "selah". This might be tempting, since it is not an English word and therefore could be counted as not part of the English text of the poem. In fact "selah" poses something of a problem for scholars: it is part of the original Hebrew text of the psalms, but is generally left untranslated, because we do not really know what it means. When dealing with a language like Ancient Hebrew, which has not been continually written and spoken across the centuries, and which only bequeathed us a limited collection of texts, translations involve a certain amount of deduction and educated guess-work. We can look at other ancient languages in the same part of the world, and hope to see connections or words whose meaning we know which might be similar enough to allow us to speculate, but this is not an exact science.

In the case of "selah" scholars are fairly certain the word is related to the original setting of the psalms, as songs or chants used in the religious worship of Ancient Israel. The text which accompanies the psalms themselves mentions singers and directors of music, and many believe that "selah" is a marking telling the singers something about the way the psalm should be performed. It might be an instruction about how to chant the poem, or to pause at that point for an instrumental passage of music. Other scholars believe it is an instruction to the audience rather than the performer, the equivalent of saying "pay attention, and reflect upon what you have heard". It is possible to compare this to another untranslated word regularly used in more modern worship: "amen". Though different in meaning, it also rounds off a passage of religious worship with an unusual and archaic word, which the listeners understand relates to what they have heard and what it means. These theories present different ideas about the possible meanings of "selah", but they all regard it as definitely part of the psalm's text. If indeed it is a musical notation, the equivalent of a treble clef or a rest, then there might be some justification for ignoring it and counting "spear" as the 46th word. Unfortunately for the legend, we do not have sufficient evidence to dismiss the word. Even more unfortunately, there is even less evidence that the translators and printers of the King James Bible regarded "selah" as a disposable word either. It is printed in the same font and the same size as all the other words of the psalm, without being separated or marked out in any way.

The King James Bible does print some letters and words in unusual ways, so we know that the people involved in creating it were used to the idea of signalling to readers that particular words had an unusual status. The first letters of the psalms, for example, are printed with elaborate decorations rather like the beginning of illuminated manuscripts. Some words are printed in italics, since translating from one language to another is never a precise and objective process, and the translators wanted to make it clear when they had added English words to bring out the meaning of the line. For example, "And David stayed *in* the city, and it *was* safe for three years" shows that the Hebrew text did not include "in" or "was", but that these are necessary in English to show what the passage means. Another example of marking out a word is the use of all capital letters for the word "lord" when it refers to God. Thus the two phrases "the armies of the

Lords of the North" and "thus saith the LORD" are printed differently, as I've done here. This is to mark the places where the original Hebrew text has the Tetragrammaton, the four letters understood to represent the name of God, but which were almost never pronounced aloud in Ancient Israel. Anyone reading the passage out loud would substitute the word "Lord", which was understood to refer to God without actually using the sacred name, and thus English Bibles printed "LORD" to mark the fact that this was an effective translation even though the original word was not "Lord". These examples show that Early Modern Bibles, including the King James Bible, had a reasonably sophisticated system of typography which used various means to signal to readers when there was something unusual going on, some change in the flow of the text or mismatch between the original words and the way they were being represented in English. The fact that "selah" is not marked in any such way makes it clear that the translators, and presumably readers of the time, regarded it as securely part of the psalm and not an extra, spare or irrelevant word. So the legend doesn't quite match up with the text as it appeared in the King James Bible; in order to make the count work, we have to distort the text slightly.

Beyond the accuracy of the numerical position, it is worth looking at where the words "shake" and "spear" come from. Obviously in one sense they come from the original text of the psalm in Hebrew, but we can also trace the point at which the original lines were rendered into English in such a way that "shake" and "spear" appeared. The Psalm 46 legend seems to imply, even if it doesn't state specifically, that this was a choice made by the person (or people) who translated this psalm for the King James Bible. The idea of "hiding" the words seems to depend upon those words being selected particularly for the purpose. However, as I discussed in the previous chapter, the King James Bible was not a completely new translation whose wording was created for the sole purpose of his version. It was based on the previous versions of the Bible which had appeared in English, including the so-called Great Bible that appeared in the reign of Henry VIII, the Geneva Bible translated by Protestants in exile on the Continent during Mary's reign, and the Bishops' Bible issued under Elizabeth. Indeed, the translators had specific instructions to keep as close as possible to the wording of the previously accepted version. As we saw, the King James Bible was part of James' attempt to solve religious disputes within Britain and to reconcile the tensions between the Puritans and the High Church groups. A translation which appeared to be radically different from any previous version, which presented the Scriptures in drastically new words under the imprimatur of the king, would have been very unlikely to satisfy either side. The King James Bible was imagined more as a project to correct and amend the existing text. So it is no surprise to find that, when we look at other preceeding English versions, the words "shake" and "spear" already exist in Psalm 46: for example, the Geneva Bible has both words. If we go back to the 1537 Bible produced in Antwerp, the psalm reads like this:

1. In oure troubles and aduersyte, we haue founde, that God is oure refuge, oure strenght and helpe.
2. Therfore wyll we not feare, though ye erthe fell, and though the hylles were caryed in to the myddest of the see.
3. Though the waters of the see raged & were neuer so troublous, & though the mountaynes **shoke** at the tempest of the same. Selah.
4. For there is a floude, which wt his ryuers reioyseth ye citie of God, the holy dwellynge of the most hyest.
5. God is in ye myddest of her, therfore shall she not be remoued: for God helpeth her, and that ryght early.
6. The Heithen are madd, the kyngdomes make moch a doo: but when he sheweth his voyce, ye earth melteth awaye.
7. The Lorde of hostes is with vs, the God of Iacob is oure defence. Selah
8. Come hither, & beholde the workes of the Lorde, what destruccyons he hath brought vpon the earth.
9. He hath made warres to ceasse in all the worlde: he hath broken the bowe, he hath knapped the **speare** in sonder, & brent the charettes in the fyre.
10. Be still then and confesse yt I am God: I wyll be exalted amonge the Heithen, & I wyll be exalted vpon earth.
11. The Lorde of Hostes is wt vs, the God of Iacob is oure defence. Selah.

There are clear differences in the language here, and the earlier text feels much more old-fashioned. This is partly the spelling and the printing conventions, such as printing "I" for "J", and "wt" for "with", but there are also more archaic-sounding English words used in the translation. In the King James Bible, God "cutteth" the spear and "burneth" the chariot, whereas here they are "knapped" and "brent", and where the kingdoms were "moved" in the later version, here they "make moch a doo [much ado]" in a slightly quaint-sounding phrase.[8] The later version is clearly influenced by this earlier version, as we know from the historical context and can see in parallels such as "The Lord of hosts is with us; the God of Jacob is our refuge" in the King James Bible and "The Lorde of Hostes is wt vs, the God of Iacob is oure defence" in the 1537, or "God is in the midst of her; she shall not be moved: God shall help her, and that right early" and "God is in ye myddest of her, therfore shall she not be remoued: for God helpeth her, and that ryght early" in the 1537.

So the words "shoke" (or "shake") and "spear(e)" do not originate with the translators of the King James Bible. It is worth pointing out that they are not the only way to translate those Hebrew words, and there had been an English translation of Psalm 46 which used other terms: one of the version produced by 14th-century radical John Wycliffe and his followers has "troubled" for "shake" and "arms" for "spears".

To sum up, the use of "shake" and "spear" appears to be shared by the King James Bible with other English Bibles around at the time, and to have been caused by the words' appearance in earlier versions. Due to that influence, the words appear in very similar positions in these other English Bibles, which calls into doubt the significance of counting the 46th words from the beginning and the end ("selah" aside). Personally I find the historical origins of these words rather more interesting than the urban legend would suggest. It turns out that they were not smuggled in by a famous author, or included as a tribute by a fan, but instead they seem to have passed through nearly a century of English Bible translations, being preserved as the words and phrases around them were reshaped, until their coincidental appearance in the King James Bible. As I suggested earlier, it is a very modern perspective to look back and see the King James Bible and the works of Shakespeare towering over the early 17th century as the two books that mattered. Taking that view tends to obscure the other stories that we might find connected with those books, about the exiles in Geneva smuggling Bibles back into England in the hope that they would turn people's hearts towards Protestantism, or about the theatre companies having to use the names of aristocratic patrons to justify their profession, or about the king hoping his son would marry a Spanish princess and bring peace to Europe. (For literary obsessives, there are even stories to tell about which words were printed in italics, and the ongoing mystery of "selah".) Imposing a modern pattern on what's important or interesting about the past guides our attention away from what we might otherwise notice. I have been arguing that there is no significant connection between Shakespeare and the 46th Psalm, but that does not mean it is unreasonable to look for patterns in this Biblical text. On the contrary, there are definite patterns "hidden" in it, though they do not point towards Shakespeare.

Spelling out the mystery

Before delving into the patterns which can be found in the psalms, it is worth defining what we mean by the term. The psalms, like any form of literature, have a particular set of patterns and conventions within which the words are arranged. Though all literature—

especially poetry—has these kinds of conventions, the precise form they take can differ from language to language and from culture to culture. In English poetry we tend to use rhyme and a rhythm created by the emphasis falling on particular words, whereas Latin poetry relied on the length of syllables to create patterns. The poetry of the Anglo-Saxons occasionally used rhyme, but was generally built around collections of words which began with the same letters. With these they produced alliterating patterns as can be seen in these lines from the most famous surviving Anglo-Saxon poem, *Beowulf*:

> oft Scyld Scefing   sceaþena þreatum,
> monegum mægþum   meodosetla ofteah,
> egsode eorlas,   syððan ærest wearð
> feasceaft funden;   he þæs frofre gebad,
> weox under wolcnum   weorðmyndum þah,[9]

Even without knowing the language (or recognising all the letters), modern English readers can see the patterns in the letters, and can hear them if they try to read them out loud. The first line has "Scyld", "Scefing" and "sceþena", the second "monegum", "mægþum" and "meodosetla", the fourth "feasceaft", "funden" and "frofre", the fifth "weox", "wolcnum" and "weorðmyndum": the repetition of the sounds is clear. They tie the words together into recognisable units, though many of us won't know what those words or those units mean without some further study. Nonetheless, there are obviously rules and conventions underpinning the poetry here, and the more the audience understands about those rules, the more they can appreciate the artistry of the poet. The author's selection and rearrangement of words into artistic patterns is part of what we enjoy about poetry, especially when those patterns are slightly rigid or difficult to handle, like a sonnet. Perhaps even more, we enjoy seeing where they test, bend or break the rules which govern the usual patterns, though of course we can only appreciate this kind of artistry if we already know the rules and have read a lot of poetry which follows them. The poetry which appears in the Hebrew Bible appears to have its own set of poetic conventions and patterns, though scholars continue to disagree about the details of them. In brief, there seem to be metrical patterns, which involve the arrangement of stressed syllables into recognisable shapes, some use of rhyme, a distinctively "poetic" style of writing which involves ambiguity and the missing out of unimportant words, and the technique of "parallelism".[10] This last feature is the only one which consistently survives most translations into English lines, and which can be heard in the early English Bibles and ever since. Essentially it involves lines being grouped into pairs, with the first line making a statement, and the second replying to it somehow. This might involve repeating the statement in different words, extending or modifying the statement, contradicting it, making another statement which puts different things in the same grammatical positions, or another form of response. It is easier to see in practice, as in these examples from the King James Bible:

> Give ear to my words, O Lord,
> consider my meditation.[11]

> O Lord, rebuke me not in thine anger,
> neither chasten me in thy hot displeasure.[12]

> Lord, who shall abide in thy tabernacle?
> Who shall dwell in thy holy hill?[13]

> Let my sentence come forth from thy presence;
> Let thine eyes behold the things that are equal.[14]

> The heavens declare the glory of God;
> and the firmament sheweth his handwork[15]

There is still considerable academic disagreement about the kinds of parallelism which exist, whether there is a single set of patterns which governs the poetry of the Hebrew Bible, where the distinctions between poetry and prose should be drawn, and other questions around the issue. Nonetheless, it is fair to say that parallelism as a poetic technique is audible in the English Bibles of Shakespeare's time, but had not been theorised by the scholars of the time. (That took place in the 18th century, with Robert Lowth's *Lectures on the Sacred Poetry of the Hebrews*.)

If these are the basic patterns of psalm poetry, which don't necessarily provide a "message" in themselves, but rather tie the words together and set up structures within which meaning can be developed and explored, there are also less obvious patterns to be found in the psalms. For example, a number of them are arranged as acrostics in the original Hebrew, with the first letters of each line following a pre-determined pattern. This is often an alphabetical sequence, working its way through the letters in a way which becomes clear in this English version of Psalm 37, which was translated to deliberately reproduce the pattern:

> Agree not to fret yourself because of the
> wicked,
> be not envious of wrongdoers!
> Be confident in the LORD, and do good;
> so you will dwell in the land, and enjoy
> security.
> Commit your way to the LORD;
> trust in him and he will act.
> Do not worry about the LORD's deeds
> but wait patiently for him.[16]

Some scholars have taken this as proof that some of the psalm's meaning was intended to appear when the text was read rather than spoken or sung, since the acrostic pattern is much more obvious to the eye than the ear. It requires a much more attentive and analytical listener to mentally note the first letter of each line, and relate that to the first letter of the next lines, and notice the pattern. The resulting awareness of the pattern is almost certainly less likely to register on an instinctive level than the rhyme or the alliteration of other poetry. Other scholars believe that listeners steeped in the poems and their various forms would be able to detect, enjoy and reflect upon the acrostic connections. Indeed, the book of Psalms appears to use acrostics to convey a religious meaning: the use of the alphabetical structure in psalms seems to connect with the idea that the world is ordered by God, and the devout person can align themselves with that harmony. The use of the alphabet, implicitly containing all the possibilities of all words, to order a poem within the Scriptures, displays what William P. Brown calls an "interest in ordering life and living lives in line with the divine order".[17] (This notion of mystically mapping the alphabet onto the whole of reality reappears most obviously in the New Testament in the description of Christ in Revelation 22:13 as "the Alpha and Omega, the first and the last, the beginning and the end", based on the fact that alpha and omega are the letters at either end of the Greek alphabet.) Psalm 145 even reproduces this acrostic pattern based on the alphabet and then deliberately breaks it halfway through, apparently in order to produce a more sophisticated meaning. In English this psalm begins

> I will exalt you, my God the King;
> I will praise your name for ever and ever.
> Every day I will praise you
> and extol your name for ever and ever.

As it continues, Psalm 145 spells out various attributes of God, including faithfulness, greatness, goodness, and particularly God's "dominion" and "kingdom". As Susan

Gillingham points out, in the Hebrew version the lines follow the acrostic sequence through the alphabet, but a few lines in the middle are shuffled around, disrupting the pattern.[18] Instead of running "k-l-m" the beginning of these lines run "m-l-k". Though it might be even less noticeable in performance than the main alphabetical pattern, this disruption may well be intentional, since "melek" means "king" in Hebrew, and the psalm's major theme is the kingship of God. Both the overall pattern of the acrostic, and this small breaking of the pattern, contribute to the psalm's reflection on the nature of God. This is exactly the kind of "hidden message" which we might hope to find, if we believed in the Psalm 46 legend, since it involves the shifting around of words within specific positions to spell out another word which is only legible when the correct sequence is understood. Given that Psalm 145 appears to have a complex and obscure word-pattern concealed within it in the original Hebrew, it is not unreasonable to think that the translators might have found it appropriate to produce their own word patterns. Unfortunately for the legend, reading the King James Bible's version of Psalm 145 does not demonstrate any attempt to reproduce the acrostic structure:

1. I will extol thee, my God, O king; and I will bless thy name for ever and ever.
2. Every day will I bless thee; and I will praise thy name for ever and ever.
3. Great is the Lord, and greatly to be praised; and his greatness is unsearchable.
4. One generation shall praise thy works to another, and shall declare thy mighty acts.
5. I will speak of the glorious honour of thy majesty, and of thy wondrous works.
6. And men shall speak of the might of thy terrible acts: and I will declare thy greatness.
7. They shall abundantly utter the memory of thy great goodness, and shall sing of thy righteousness.
8. The Lord is gracious, and full of compassion; slow to anger, and of great mercy.
9. The Lord is good to all: and his tender mercies are over all his works.
10. All thy works shall praise thee, O Lord; and thy saints shall bless thee.
11. They shall speak of the glory of thy kingdom, and talk of thy power;
12. To make known to the sons of men his mighty acts, and the glorious majesty of his kingdom.
13. Thy kingdom is an everlasting kingdom, and thy dominion endureth throughout all generations.
14. The Lord upholdeth all that fall, and raiseth up all those that be bowed down.
15. The eyes of all wait upon thee; and thou givest them their meat in due season.
16. Thou openest thine hand, and satisfiest the desire of every living thing.
17. The Lord is righteous in all his ways, and holy in all his works.

18. The Lord is nigh unto all them that call upon him, to all that call upon him in truth.
19. He will fulfil the desire of them that fear him: he also will hear their cry, and will save them.
20. The Lord preserveth all them that love him: but all the wicked will he destroy.
21. My mouth shall speak the praise of the Lord: and let all flesh bless his holy name for ever and ever.

In order to maintain the meaning of the words, and cast them into a meaningful set of English phrases, the acrostic pattern has been abandoned. Speakers of Latin might be encouraged by the fact that making an acrostic of the beginning of the lines starts with the exciting words "I, EGO", as if the person behind the translation were declaring themselves to the reader with an egotistical flourish before beginning to transmit their message. However, if the attempt continues, the letters jumble into nonsense, and dissolve near the end into a sequence of Ts which don't seem likely to mean anything in any language. If there is a message in the opening letters of verses 10–18, it is one that can only be explained by a combination of dictation to a scribe and an unfortunate stutter. Less frivolously, it is not surprising that translating this psalm from Hebrew to English disrupted the acrostic pattern and introduced a preponderance of "T" into the first position of each line. One of the major characteristics of the poetry of the Psalms, from the linguistic point of view, is the compressed style which misses out minor words in favour of vivid images. The much more expansive English version has to add words like "is", "and", "that" and "the" in order to make the poetic phrases comprehensible and logical for modern readers. Added to which, as mentioned above, the sacred name of God is translated into the English of the King James Bible as "The LORD". Therefore many more lines would naturally begin with the word "The", whether as part of the name of God or simply as the definite article which appears alongside so many nouns in English. After examining the possibilities of hidden messages within the psalms, and acknowledging that there are indeed patterns woven into the word choice and word placement in the original Hebrew text, we have to conclude that there is no support here for the Psalm 46 legend.

Where's there a Will?

It is not unreasonable either to think that Shakespeare might have chosen to hide his name within a poem, even though I do not believe he did so in Psalm 46. The word "will" appears as a pun in several of Shakespeare's sonnets, most notably in Sonnet 135, below:

> Whoever hath her wish, thou hast thy Will,
> And Will to boot, and Will in over-plus;
> More than enough am I that vexes thee still,
> To thy sweet will making addition thus.
> Wilt thou, whose will is large and spacious,
> Not once vouchsafe to hide my will in thine?
> Shall will in others seem right gracious,
> And in my will no fair acceptance shine?
> The sea, all water, yet receives rain still,
> And in abundance addeth to his store;
> So thou, being rich in Will, add to thy Will
> One will of mine, to make thy large will more.
> Let no unkind, no fair beseechers kill;
> Think all but one, and me in that one Will.

Despite the variability of punctuation in Early Modern printed texts, which makes it difficult to know how far the capitalisation of first letters is either deliberate (and if so, whether it originates with the author), there is clearly a lot going on in this poem around the word "will". The first line puns on the connection between the abstract noun "will", meaning "intention, thing wished for" and Shakespeare's first name. Throughout the poem there is also another pun, based on the fact that in the language of the time "will" meaning "wish or desire" has a specifically sexual meaning. Rather in the same way that "desire" in modern English can mean a desire for lasagne or a desire for a better world, but when used without any modification is usually understood to mean "desire" in the sexual sense, "will" strongly implied sexual longing and lust. Along with this implication came another, cruder and more straightforward meaning: in Early Modern slang, "will" could refer to either the male or female genitals. With this in mind, "Wilt thou, whose will is large and spacious,/ Not once vouchsafe to hide my will in thine?" involves a series of puns, ranging from "can our intentions about our lives not align with each other?", through "can't your erotic appetite fold itself into mine?", to "can't I insert my genitals into yours?" The poem ranges energetically across these various implications, connecting the name of the writer to his sexual desire, the beloved's sexual experience to her will for power, the auxiliary verb "will" to a reasonably obvious dick joke, and so on. Elsewhere in the sonnets similar, though less extended, puns appear on the word, including sonnet 136, which ends with the lines

> Make but my name thy love, and love that still,
> And then thou lovest me for my name is Will.

As Paul Edmondson and Stanley Wells point out, amidst the intricacies of capitalisation and verbal interplay which call into question the precise meanings which are being articulated here at any particular moment, the poem does actually end with the words "my name is Will".[19] Shakespeare clearly wasn't averse to "hiding" his name in his poetry, though "hide" is probably the wrong word to use. In the examples here the name is working on multiple levels of meaning, signalling both the writer's identity and various other implications of the word "will". Some connection, if only a basic pun, is produced. In the Psalm 46 legend, no such wordplay is suggested: the presence of "shake" and "spear" does not produce a pun or a multiple meaning, deepening or complicating the sense of the line, but simply advertises to the person counting words that "Shakespeare was here". We should also note that the sonnets were published at Shakespeare's own instigation—unlike his plays—and included his name on the title page. The wordplay in the sonnets begins with the reader knowing that a man called "Will" wrote these poems, and using that knowledge to enjoy the interplay of meanings.[20] Shakespeare is not signing his work by flinging around the word "Will" in this way, but rather playing on the audience's existing awareness of his authorship. It's a rather different way of "hiding" a name inside the poem. So it makes sense to be alert for Shakespeare's own name in his texts, and we can see him playing with it in Sonnet 135, but this doesn't add any particular support to the Psalm 46 legend.

The Textual Verdict

As I've suggested in this chapter, a close examination of the text of Psalm 46, and of other texts surrounding it, does not support the Psalm 46 legend. However, this does not mean that we should give up paying minute attention to the details of Biblical and Shakespearean texts. There are plenty of intricate meanings to be explored, from the acrostics of the Hebrew Psalms to the dirty wordplay of the Sonnets, and the poets of the past clearly valued the possibilities of producing meaning by the form of their works as well as the words which constituted them. In fact, as I hope the textual analysis above has suggested, the Psalm 46 legend is rather too modest in its ambitions for the secret pattern it claims to have discovered. It suggests that the hidden words simply point to the author who translated the psalm, rather than complicating the poem's meaning, making an implicit statement about the structure of the world, connecting two ideas together or indulging in elaborate wordplay. After examining the texts of the Psalms and the Sonnets, we might think that the Psalm 46 legend fails not because it want us to believe too much about the obscure meanings of this particular poem, but because it wants us to believe too little.

The next chapter will develop this possibility, by examining the problems with the legend from a poetic point of view, comparing Psalm 46 in the King James Bible with other translations, and exploring the place of the psalms in the literary world of Early Modern England.

The Theory and the Poetry

Having explored the historical context of Shakespeare's plays and the translation of the King James Bible, and delved into the specific texts involved, I'd now like to consider the Psalm 46 legend from the point of view of poetry. Literary judgements have less of the objective quality we ascribe to historical facts, and an argument from the poetic (or otherwise) qualities of a text might seem a rather dubious basis for discrediting the legend. However, exploring the literary and historical context of the Psalms as poetry in this era sheds more light on the claims the legend makes. As in the previous two chapters, I believe that this angle of investigation opens up far more absorbing issues than simply whether someone hid Shakespeare's name in the text.

Signing Shakespeare's Own Name

As was demonstrated in the last chapter, the way the Psalm 46 legend works is not unique to the King James Bible. Certainly the text of other versions come very close to producing the same "hidden message" when their words are counted. This does not mean that it is impossible that Shakespeare or the translators of the King James Bible decided to tweak the word order to spell "Shakespeare"—though it makes it more unlikely—but it does mean that the apparently free choice of where to put those words was rather more constrained than it might appear if they are read in isolation. It also puts a question mark over what exactly the purpose of hiding the word in the psalm might be. If we take the version of the legend in which Shakespeare himself translated Psalm 46, the story assumes that he hid the word within the poem's text in order to reveal his identity to those who read it closely enough. Aside from the historical and textual issues discussed earlier, there is a poetic problem with this theory. Psalm 46, as it appears in the King James Bible, might be a glorious piece of English poetry, but it was not composed freely or even as a poetic paraphrase of the original text. It is a careful and meticulous account of what the Hebrew text of the psalm says, based on previous translations and with additional corrections to make it more accurate. This throws doubt on exactly what Shakespeare is believed to have done with this psalm: moving a few words around and bringing the wording a bit closer to the Hebrew original is hardly a major artistic achievement. It could be extremely valuable in theological terms to make small adjustments in the text, and it was certainly in the interests of believers and clergy to have as effective and accurate a version of the psalm as possible, but the history traced so far detracts considerably from the work which a hypothetical London playwright called Shakespeare would have actually done on this poem. Put bluntly, if Shakespeare turned the Bishops' Bible text into the King James Bible text, why would he bother signing his work? His own poetry, which drew on the rich inheritance of Biblical and Classical literature, demonstrated much more talent and creativity. This is not to say that a given sonnet by Shakespeare is a better piece of poetry than a given psalm, since that would be comparing drastically different kinds of art. But the effort required to tweak the previous texts of Psalm 46 until they became the King James Bible's version is not equal to the artistic labour which produced "When to the sessions of sweet silent thought…", or "If we shadows have offended…" It is difficult to imagine Shakespeare being particularly proud of the minor word-shuffling involved. To explore this further, it is worth considering the role of the Psalms in national life at the time, and looking at the other, more poetic, versions available to Early Modern readers (and singers).

Psalms, Piety and Poetry

The Psalms were a major part of religious and literary culture in Early Modern England: what Hannibal Hamlin has called "Psalm culture" pervaded many people's experience of spirituality and creativity.[21] Weekly attendance at church was legally required of every subject (though this law was not always obeyed), and the Psalms were one of the major elements of the services, as they are in Anglican services today. Listening to the Bible read and (often) preached in church every week developed a wide Biblical literacy in the congregation, and Bible references or stories were woven through a great deal of contemporary literature. The Psalms may have been even more familiar to a lot of people, since the congregation often took part in singing them, rather than sitting and listening to them being read. The leaders and clergy of the Reformation were particularly eager that people should sing the Psalms, both because they believed strongly in active engagement with the Bible, and because the Psalms offered a religious alternative to the ballads and folk-songs sung at the time, whose content was much less edifying to their ears. The Puritans, and other strongly Protestant groups, were known for singing psalms in English translations, and Shakespeare's own characters refer to the fact.

In *The Winter's Tale* one of the rustics is preparing for the feast to celebrate the seasonal sheep-shearing, and lists music amongst the things he needs to arrange:

> "three-man song-men all, and very good ones ... one puritan amongst them, and he sings psalms to hornpipes".[22]

When the raffish knight Falstaff's plans are going awry in *1 Henry IV*, he laments "A bad world, I say. I would I were a weaver, I could sing psalms, or anything."[23] Falstaff refers here to the Huguenot weavers who had left the Continent because of religious persecution, and were famous for singing psalms to the rhythm of the shuttles as they sat at their looms. Falstaff seems to be suggesting that he is so depressed and harried by the world, he can see no further prospect of enjoying life and so might as well turn religious and sit singing psalms with the weavers, or perhaps that the lamentations expressed in many psalms feel suitable to his outlook on things.

The psalms to which these passages refer were almost certainly "metrical psalms", or versions which altered the lines into recognisable poetic form in English. As I discussed in an earlier chapter, the Hebrew Psalms have their own poetic form, structured around two-part statements and responses. When translated into English, this can produce impressive and moving lines, but it does not immediately sound like any poetic form generally used in the language during Shakespeare's lifetime. It lacks the kinds of rhythm and rhyme which we are used to hearing in English verse, and which were even more expected in the Early Modern era. To make the Psalms memorable and singable, Protestants translated them into "metrical psalms", so called because they fit the lines to a particular poetic metre. The most famous example of this was the Sternhold and Hopkins Psalter, published in the later 16th century and named after Thomas Sternhold and John Hopkins, who translated most of the contents. This Psalter sounds rather basic and crude as poetry, especially when compared to the great poets of the time such as Edmund Spenser, Philip Sidney or Shakespeare, but it did provide a singable text of the Psalms for general use. This is how the Sternhold and Hopkins Psalter renders the 46th Psalm:

> The Lord is our defence and aid,
> > the strength whereby we stand:
> When we with woe are much dismay'd,
> > he is our help at hand.
> Tho' the earth move we will not fear,
> > tho' mountains high and steep,
> Be thrust and hurled here and there
> > within the sea so deep.
> No, tho' the Sea do rage so sore,
> > that all the banks it spills:
> And though it overflow the shore,
> > and beat down mighty hills.
> For one fair floor doth send abroad
> > his pleasant streams apace,
> To fresh the City of our God,
> > and wash his holy place.
> In midst of her the Lord doth dwell
> > she can no whit decay:
> All things against her that rebel,
> > the Lord will surely slay.

> The heathen folk and kingdoms fear,
>   the people make a noise:
> The earth do melt and not appear,
>   when God puts forth his voice.
> The Lord of hosts doth take our part,
>   to us he hath an eye:
> Our hope of health with all our heart
>   on Jacob's God doth lie.
> Come here and see with mind and thought
>   the workings of our God:
> What wonders he himself hath wrought
>   in all the world abroad.
> By him all wars are husht and gone
>   though countries did conspire:
> Their bows and spears he brake each one,
>   their Chariots burnt with fire.
> Be still, therefore, and know that I
>   am God, and therefore will,
> Among the heathen people be
>   high exalted still.
> The Lord of hosts doth us defend,
>   he is our strength and tower:
> On Jacob's God we do depend,
>   and on his might and power.[24]

As can be seen by a comparison with the King James Bible or Bishops' Bible text, this version is careful to keep both the overall meaning of the poem, and the individual contents of each line. Though the words are shuffled around to produce a regular rhythm and a set of rhymes, each couple of lines is recognisably a rendering of the equivalent passage in Psalm 46. Very little poetic "licence" is taken in moving ideas around, changing images or altering the statements made by the text it is based upon. This is because the point of this Psalter was not to produce new and elegant poetry but to shape the words of the Psalms into verses that would stick in the memory and flow from the lips of the people of England. Given the emphasis the Protestants put on increased access to the Bible, it would have been counterproductive to produce a set of verses which did not help people in getting to know what the Bible actually said, and to memorise its words. It is this concern to be faithful (in various senses) which sets the agenda for the Sternhold and Hopkins Psalter, and which surely contributes to the rather wooden and pedestrian sound its psalms have to an ear used to the lyrics of the same era. It must be admitted, however, that despite that obvious lack in refined poetic quality, the Sternhold and Hopkins version is more recognisably English poetry than the King James Bible version. The first three lines of the latter, quoted before, run thus:

> God is our refuge and strength, a very present
> help in trouble.
> Therefore will not we fear, though the earth be
> removed, and though the mountains be carried
> into the midst of the sea.

> The Lord is our defence and aid,
> the strength whereby we stand:
> When we with woe are much dismay'd,
> he is our help at hand.
> Tho' the earth move we will not fear,
> tho' mountains high and steep,
> Be thrust and hurled here and there
> within the sea so deep.

The sweeping lines of the King James Bible are majestic and impressive, and the repetition in "though the earth be moved … though the mountains be carried" signals that this is a deliberately-wrought piece of writing. The Sternhold and Hopkins however, with its regular alternation of eight-syllable lines with six-syllables lines, and its rhymes, is much more obviously poetry. It has arranged the words into the regular pulse of iambic metre, the rhythmic form which sustains so much poetry in English, and which comes in two-syllable units with an unstressed syllable followed by a stressed syllable. Just reading the opening lines casually one can hear this pulse: "The LORD is OUR deFENCE and AID/ the STRENGTH whereBY we STAND." No such rhythm is evident when reading out "God is our refuge and strength, a very present help in trouble." Reading the two next to each other, we might come to the paradoxical-sounding conclusion that the King James Bible rendering sounds more authentically "poetic", but the Sternhold and Hopkins version is more obviously "poetry".

Taking another step further away from straightforward translation (as much as translating poetry from Ancient Hebrew into 16th-century English could ever be straightforward) towards poetry, we find another poet of the time who produced their own version of Psalm 46. Lady Mary Sidney was an aristocratic writer of the 16th century, and part of an erudite and staunchly Protestant social circle. She and her brother Philip translated whole sequences of the Psalms into English poetry, taking a somewhat freer and more literary approach to the material. This is her rendering of the 46th psalm:

> God gives us strength, and keeps us sound,
> A present help when dangers call;
> Then fear not we, let quake the ground,
> And into seas let mountains fall,
> Yea, so let seas withal,
> In wat'ry hills arise,
> And may the earthly hills appal,
> With dread and dashing cries.

For, lo, a river streaming joy
With purling murmur safely slides,
That city washing from annoy,
In holy shrine where God resides.
God in her centre bides:
What can this city shake?
God early aids and ever guides:
Who can this city take?

When nations go against her bent,
And kings with siege her walls enround:
The void of air his voice doth rent,
Earth fails their feet with melting ground.
To strength and keep us sound,
The God of armies arms:
Our rock on Jacob's God we found
Above the reach of harms.

Oh, come with me, oh, come and view
The trophies of Jehovah's hand:
What wracks from him our foes pursue,
How clearly he hath purged our land.
By him wars silent stand:
He brake the archer's bow,
Made chariot's wheel a fi'ry brand,
And spear to shivers go.

"Be still", saith he; "know, God am I:
Know I will be with conquest crowned,
Above all nations raisèd high,
High raised above this earthly round."
To strength and keep us sound,
The God of armies arms:
Our rock on Jacob's God we found,
Above the reach of harms.[25]

This is significantly more sophisticated in poetic terms than the Sternhold and Hopkins version, as well as being a freer version of the text. Where their verse has the regular to-and-fro of eight-syllable lines followed by six-syllable lines, Sidney provides a more varied pattern. She creates stanzas of eight lines each, split into two sections, with these numbers of syllables: 8 8 8 8 – 6 6 8 6. The two sections of the stanza are tied together by rhyme sounds which produce the pattern A B A B – B C B C. The combination of repetition and variation across rhymes and line lengths produces a subtle but harmonious pattern, which looks somewhat awkward and mechanical when tabulated (as I have just done) but which can both heard and felt when the poem is read out loud. Sidney's poetic technique is evident in other aspects of the poem, such as the opening line which is repeated in modified form in the middle and final stanzas. "God gives us strength and keeps us sound" becomes "to strength and keep us sound" in the later stanzas, recasting "strength" from a noun to a verb in a piece of poetic compression. This kind of verbal invention is visible again in the phrase "The God of armies arms", in which Sidney renders the tradition epithet "the Lord of hosts" in a more direct way, and pairs it with the verb "to arm" meaning to take up weapons and put on armour. Likewise the chiasmic structure in the last stanza, in which she ends one line with "raisèd high" and begins the next with "High raised", repeating the words but reversing their order and shifting the number of syllables in the phrase from three to two. Once again, when spelled out in this way these devices may sound pedantic and technical, but in performance they add a level of complexity and intricacy to the flow of the words.

Sidney's freedom in rendering the text appears in more extended form in the first stanza, as the notion of the mountains crumbling into the sea from the psalm text becomes the basis for a metaphor in hers:

> And into seas let mountains fall,
> Yea, so let seas withal,
> In wat'ry hills arise,
> And may the earthly hills appal,
> With dread and dashing cries.[26]

The seas themselves become hill-like as they swell up, and the terrifying confusion of water and land which remains only implicit in the earlier text is teased out into an image of the hills being faced by an eerie double of themselves produced by the water. The vigour which results from this rearrangement of the text's ideas is matched by the shift she engineers in the poem's voice and tone. Out of the stoicism of the psalm text, which assures the reader of God's faithfulness although terrible things should happen, Sidney develops an active bravado which dares the world to descend into chaos: "let mountains fall … let seas". She adds rhetorical questions: "What can this city shake? … Who can this city take?", and addresses the reader directly, exclaiming "Oh, come with me, oh come and view…" All these changes give Sidney's poem a more urgent and dynamic feeling, engaging the subject of the lines and the reader with a livelier diction.

All of this may not convince any given reader that Sidney's poem is "better" as poetry than Sternhold and Hopkins' version. I think it undoubtedly is, and I think that becomes evident by simply reading the poem. Sidney's lines are at once more intricate and more flowing, they seem to strain less in getting the words into place so they fit the metre and the rhyme scheme.

The resulting poem feels more like a complete aesthetic and spiritual statement in which the ideas have been elaborated, tested and restated in satisfying ways whilst the rhythmic and sonic patterns of the verse work themselves out. To which statements anyone might reasonably respond "No they aren't, and it doesn't feel like that to me." What is more objectively provable, though, is that Sidney's work is less like a phrase-for-phrase translation which has been shunted into lines of verse, and more like a poem based upon the psalm. It is still strongly based on the images and meanings of the psalm text, and could potentially serve the same purpose as Sternhold and Hopkins' Psalm 46, in giving people a memorable and accessible English version of the psalm. Nonetheless, it looks more like a poet taking inspiration from the psalm, and shows what a great Renaissance lyric poet could do with the Psalms, whilst staying close to the earlier text. It is worth noting that the Sidney siblings' poetic translations of the Psalms are presented in a wide range of different poetic forms; in fact, the same form is only repeated a few times. They were deliberately exploring the various possible ways of constructing metre and rhyme in English poetry, foregrounding the technical and formal aspects of verse. This can be seen in Mary's version of Psalm 102, which I have placed next to the version which appears in the King James Bible:

1. Hear my prayer, O Lord, and let my cry come unto thee.
2. Hide not thy face from me in the day when I am in trouble; incline thine ear unto me: in the day when I call answer me speedily.
3. For my days are consumed like smoke, and my bones are burned as an hearth.
4. My heart is smitten, and withered like grass; so that I forget to eat my bread.

Sidney renders these lines thus:

> O Lord, my praying hear;
> Lord, let my cry come to thine ear.
> Hide not thy face away,
> But haste, and answer me,
> In this my most, most miserable day,
> Wherein I pray and cry to thee.
>
> My days as smoke are past;
> My bones as flaming fuel waste,
> Mown down in me, alas,
> With scythe of sharpest pain.
> My heart is withered like the wounded grass;
> My stomach doth all food disdain.

Four lines of imposing and balanced Hebrew poetry become two six-line stanzas of lively, agile and plaintive lyric. As Susan Gillingham points out, part of the impulse behind Sidney's translations was her dissatisfaction with the lack of ornament and poetic style in the Coverdale and Geneva versions of the Psalms, and these poems amply remedy that lack.[27]

The formal experiments also connected form with the overall meaning of individual psalms. Thus when she came to translate psalms which dealt with heroic or royal subjects, Sidney rendered them in the hexameter used in Classical and English poetry for these modes. Her version of Psalm 100 is cast in a form rather better-known to modern readers than heroic hexameter: a sonnet.

> O all you lands, the treasures of your joy,
> In merry shout upon the Lord bestow:
> Your service cheerfully on him employ,
> With triumph song into his presence go.
> Know first that he is God; and after know
> This God did us, not we ourselves create:
> We are his flock, for us his feedings grow;
> We are his folk, and he upholds our state.
> With thankfulness, oh, enter then his gate:
> Make through each porch of his your praises
>   ring.

> All good, all grace, of his high name relate,
> He of all grace and goodness is the spring.
> Time in no terms his mercy comprehends;
> From age to age his truth itself extends.

If this psalm seems both familiar to some readers, and a little wrong somehow, it may be because a much more famous translation of this psalm (also originating in the 16th century) is still sung today, but in a different metre. "All People That On Earth Do Dwell", from the psalter produced by English Protestant exiles in Geneva, runs like this:

> All people that on earth do dwell,
> sing to the Lord with cheerful voice;
> him serve with mirth, his praise forth tell.
> Come ye before him and rejoice.
>
> Know that the Lord is God indeed;
> without our aid he did us make;
> we are his folk; he doth us feed,
> and for his sheep he doth us take.
>
> O enter then his gates with praise;
> approach with joy his courts unto;
> praise, laud, and bless his name always,
> for it is seemly so to do.
>
> For why? The Lord our God is good;
> his mercy is forever sure;
> his truth at all times firmly stood,
> and shall from age to age endure.

There are various modernised versions of this hymn which tend to alter the archaic elements like the phrasing of "him serve with mirth, his praise forth tell" or the rhetorical question of "For why? The Lord our God is good", and it is usually sung to one of the most widely-known tunes in English-speaking Christianity. The tune itself, which originated amongst the Protestants of Geneva, is known as "Old Hundredth", because of its association with this version of Psalm 100, and because of its regular eight-syllable measures and memorable tune it is used to sing a number of other songs (though not Sidney's Psalm 100). Church musicians to this day can sometimes be heard introducing a new hymn to the congregation by saying "We'll sing it to Old Hundredth."

Sidney's translations also drew on her knowledge of the patterns with which the Psalms had been composed and interlinked, as can be seen in her rendering of the very short Psalm 117. It appears in the King James Bible as:

> O praise the Lord, all ye nations: praise him, all ye people.
> For his merciful kindness is great toward us: and the truth of the Lord endureth for ever. Praise ye the Lord.

In Sidney's version, it is considerably expanded, though via unusual and short lines:

> **P**raise him that aye
> **R**emains the same:
> **A**ll tongues display
> **I**ehovah's fame.
> **S**ing all that share
> **T**his earthly ball:
> **H**is mercies are
> **E**xposed to all:
> **L**ike as the word
> **O**nce he doth give,
> **R**olled in record,
> **D**oth time outlive.

The rationale behind the form of this expansion becomes clear if a reader notices the first letter of each line, reading vertically down the page: Sidney has embedded an acrostic which reads P-R-A-I-S-T-H-E-L-O-R-D. Her psalm poems are at once deeply religious engagements with the Biblical texts, daring technical experiments with the possibilities of the English language and poetic forms, and a probing of the connection between form and meaning. Part of the point in my exploring them here is to show what a poet of Sidney's ability could do when tackling the Psalms, and the striking poems which resulted. It contributes to my argument that very few people reading the Psalms in the King James Bible would have thought of them as sophisticated and dramatic poetry, certainly not as English poems by an accomplished poet.

If Mary Sidney's poetic psalms show one form of elaborate literary engagement with the Biblical texts, Edmund Spenser's love sonnets provide another example. Spenser was part of the same literary and political circles as Sidney, though he spent a significant portion of his career in official posts in Ireland. His sonnet sequence *Amoretti* was addressed to his second wife, Elizabeth Boyle, and details the courtship leading up to their marriage (which he marked by the connected poem *Epithalamion*). One particular feature of Spenser's poems in the *Amoretti*, which has caused literary critics to investigate them closely, is their specificity: whole runs of the 89 poems are intended to be associated with specific dates during the months leading up to the couple's wedding in the summer of 1594. Spenser uses these dates to connect the poems with the readings set for particular days in the Book of Common Prayer. As William Johnson notes, Sonnet 46 in the sequence, "When my abode's prefixed time is spent", corresponds with the day on which Psalm

46 was the first reading.[28] Looking closely at this poem reveals a sophisticated literary engagement with the imagery and tone of the psalm.

> When my abode's prefixed time is spent,
> My cruel fair straight bids me wend my way:
> But then from heaven most hideous storms are sent,
> As willing me against her will to stay.
> Whom then shall I—or heaven, or her—obey?
> The heavens know best what is the best for me:
> But as she will, whose will my life doth sway,
> My lower heaven, so it perforce must be.
> But ye high heavens, that all this sorrow see,
> Sith all your tempests cannot hold me back,
> Assuage your storms, or else both you and she
> Will both together me too sorely wrack.
> Enough it is for one man to sustain
> The storms which she alone on me doth rain.[29]

The narrative of the poem, to briefly paraphrase, involves Spenser as an ardent lover who has been spending enjoyable time with the lady he is courting. When the time appointed for the visit has run out, she expects him to leave, but he hesitates because a storm of rain has appeared. Stuck between disobeying his mistress and braving the storm, he calls upon the heavens to stop the rain. It is an elegant, flippant poem which takes a small incident and makes a mock-dramatic scenario from it. Indeed this might be one of the most stereotypically British poems of the Renaissance, since it is essentially a sonnet complaining about the weather. Spenser draws on some poetic tropes familiar from the French "courtly love" literature of the Middle Ages, and the more recent Italian love poetry of Petrarch: the idea of the beloved woman as a tyrannical mistress whom the lover must obey and the notion that the movements of nature (such as the weather) can be interpreted as messages or states of emotion. The result, in the poem, is a scenario where the poet is caught between obeying his lover and obeying the weather, in an emotional state memorably dramatised several centuries later in The Clash's "Should I Stay Or Should I Go?"

These tropes are complicated by the poem's implicit relationship to the psalm set for the day. This would not necessarily come to mind without the ongoing connection to the Book of Common Prayer which the sonnet sequence provides, but once we are aware of that relationship it can influence the poem's meaning for readers. The major connection is the storm imagery which appears in both texts. The psalm celebrates the fact that God is steadfast and reliable even in the midst of storms and tempests, and will keep his people safe when water engulfs everything, whilst the sonnet irreverently suggests the storm has been sent by divine providence to give him more time with his beloved. In both God's goodness is demonstrated via the storm, though to very different ends Indeed in the sonnet Spenser declares that he will have to leave, even though "the heavens" have tried to keep him there, because although "The heavens know best what is the best for me", his mistress controls the "lower heaven" of his romantic hopes. There may be some of the same sexual punning that Shakespeare's sonnet about "will" displayed, since Spenser comments that:

> But as she will, whose will my life doth sway,
> My lower heaven, so it perforce must be.

As discussed in an earlier chapter, "will" could have a range of meanings from "wish" or "intention", through "desire" to crude sexual references. The beloved's "will", which controls Spenser's behaviour, may be interpreted as her wishes as expressed in her instructions to him, or may be read as a bawdy implication about the "lower heaven" which Spenser one day hopes to enjoy. The poem engages with the psalm at quite some distance, both in terms of text and tone, riffing on the storm imagery and the idea of God's power to produce an echo of the devotional text in its own witty elaboration of romantic love.

Thus there were a whole range of poetic engagements with the Psalms in the 16th and 17th centuries, from translations and metrical psalms, to poetic experiments and irreverent poetic riffs. The Psalms were a major influence on the literature of the period, and shaped the work of many poets in powerful and lasting ways. They also provided a wealth of poetic material for those who weren't poets, but who sang them as they would have sung ballads or folk songs. I've presented these examples above to show that Psalm 46 in the King James Bible, though poetic and impressive, wouldn't have been regarded as English poetry in the same way as Shakespeare's own lyrics, or the poetry of Sidney and Spenser would have been. This provides more evidence, I believe, that the Psalm 46 legend is untrue, but it has also been an excuse to look at some inventive and enjoyable poetry along the way. I'd now like to turn to Shakespeare's own involvement with the Bible. Although (I would argue) he did not contribute to the King James Bible, Shakespeare's works are steeped in the Bible's stories and imagery. Though some of this book so far has argued that there was a considerable distance between the theatre and the Church, there is certainly a rich and complex relationship between Shakespeare and the English Bible, and one which illuminates his works in fascinating ways.

Shakespeare and the Bible(s)

The influence of the Bible on Shakespeare's works was first studied in depth in the mid to late 19th century. The titles of books such as T.R. Eaton's *Shakespeare and the Bible: showing how much the great dramatist was indebted to Holy Writ for his profound knowledge of human nature* suggest how this scholarship was part of an attempt to fashion Shakespeare into a suitably religious figure.[30] The impulse behind tracing Shakespeare's connections to the Bible, for many Victorians, seems to have been a desire to claim him as a distinctively Christian and devout writer, rather than one who simply wrote at a time when Christianity was an inherent part of everyday life and culture. Some early 20th-century literary critics reacted against this tendency, with the eminent scholar Sidney Lee declaring that:

> references to scriptural characters and incidents are not conspicuous in Shakespeare's plays, but, such as they are, they ... indicate that general acquaintance with the narrative of both Old and New Testaments which a clever boy would be certain to acquire either in the schoolroom of at church on Sundays.[31]

In stressing the apparent influence of the Bible on Shakespeare's "early development" and denying it was proof of "close and continuous study of the Bible in adult life", Lee attempted to downplay the importance of Christianity in Shakespeare's mental world and literary works. Essentially, he was suggesting that Shakespeare grew out of reading the Bible, and that his artistic achievements happened in spite of, not because of, the religion which surrounded him. As we have seen elsewhere in this book, this debate over historical facts was in large part a debate over modern values, with critics producing visions of Shakespeare which validated their contemporary beliefs.

Whatever the truth about Shakespeare's personal religious faith, there is a consensus in modern scholarship that the Bible was a huge influence on his works. The standard work on the Biblical references and parallels in his plays, written in the late 1990s by Naseeb Shaheen, runs to nearly 900 pages. Close attention to the specific words used in references has allowed scholars to determine which versions of the Bible Shakespeare drew on in some cases. So, for example, Shaheen points out that when Sir Toby Belch cries out "Wilt thou set thy foot o' my neck?" to Maria in *Twelfth Night*, he is echoing Joshua 10.24: "set your feet upon the necks of these Kings: and they came near and set their feet upon their necks". The words "set thy foot" signal that the reference is to the Geneva Bible, since the other English Bibles available either have "put your feet" or "tread". Likewise, when Orlando in *As You Like It* demands "Shall I keep your hogs and eat husks with them? What prodigal portion have I spent that I should come to such penury?", he is clearly referring to the parable of the Prodigal Son, but comparing the Bible texts shows that Shakespeare had the Geneva's version of this story in mind, since only it uses the word "husks" whilst the other translations have the prodigal eating "cods".[32]

Shakespeare's engagement with the Bible includes verbal echoes, character influences and the shape of narratives or plots, though the verbal references are the easiest to identify. Even when recognised, they can be intriguing and mysterious, as in one famous example. This is a particularly apt example for my investigation of the Psalm 46 legend, since it involves both a potentially hidden name, and a dramatic proof of how important it is to understand the textual history of the English Bibles.[33] In *Midsummer Night's Dream*, Bottom wakes from his enchanted sleep near the end of the play, believing that the extraordinary events which took place in the woods near Athens—his head being changed into a donkey's, his meeting the Queen of the Fairies, etc.— have all been a bizarre dream or vision. His first impulse is to recount it, but he has some problems:

> I have had a most rare vision. I have had a dream—past the wit of man to say what dream it was. Man is but an ass if he go about to expound this dream. Methought I was—there is no man can tell what. Methought I was, and methought I had—but man is but a patched fool if he will offer to say what methought I had. The eye of man hath not heard, the ear of man hath not seen, man's hand is not able to taste, his tongue to conceive, nor his heart to report what my dream was … It shall be called "Bottom's Dream" because it hath no bottom.[34]

Bottom uses a phrase—"methought…"—which was used in the dream vision poetry of the Middle Ages, but there is also another significant echo in his speech. As Bottom declares that "the eye of man hath not heard, the ear of man hath not seen … what my dream was" he comically shows how confused the events of the play have left him, as well as speaking the literal truth. The *eye* of man has certainly not *heard* what happened to him. He has also produced a garbled version of a passage from Corinthians, which we could look up in the King James Bible:

> But as it is written, Eye hath not seen, nor ear heard, neither have entered into the heart of man, the things which God hath prepared for them that love him. But God hath revealed them unto us by his Spirit: for the Spirit searcheth all things, yea, the deep things of God.[35]

The echo is clear enough, and adds another level to Bottom's grandiloquent declaration. He is not only wondering at his supernatural exploits, but mixing up the words of the Bible in his attempt to explain just how unable he or anyone else is to explain what took place over the last few hours. However, as has been mentioned earlier in this book, Shakespeare did not grow up reading the King James Bible, and it cannot have been the source for a play written in the 1590s. If we turn to the same passage in the Great Bible, the version which would have been read at services through Shakespeare's youth, and with which he would have been much more familiar, an additional connection appears on the page:

> But it is written. The eye hath not sene, and the eare hath not hearde, nether haue entred into the herte of man, the thynges which God hath prepared for them that loue him. But god hath opened them vnto vs by his holy spirite. For the spirite searcheth all thinges, ye the botome of Gods secretes.

The appearance of the word "bottom" in this version jumps out at anyone familiar with the Shakespeare play. It is difficult to know precisely what its connection with the speech in *Midsummer Night's Dream* might be. Is it a joke hidden in the text by Shakespeare, to amuse himself and anyone sharp enough to remember the specific passage he is echoing? This need not be a joke based on readers poring over footnotes, since Shakespeare's London was a far more verbal culture than ours. Audiences were used to listening at length to speeches, plays, and sermons, to an extent which few people do now. Indeed a frequent verb used to describe attending a play was going "to hear" it, where we would usually say going "to see" it. (The same idea is still embedded in our habit of calling the people at an event the "audience", a word from the Latin *audeo* meaning "I hear", rather than "spectators", derived from *specto* meaning "I watch".) The theory that audiences might recognise this joke or reference is strengthened by the fact that the word "bottom" appears after the lines invoked by Bottom's garbled quotation. Many people in the audience, who were accustomed to listen to a preacher giving several hours of sermon, and who heard the Bible read every week at church, would be capable of completing the next couple of lines in their head, and might be amused to find the word "bottom" waiting at the end of them. They would be less likely to mentally work backwards, and find words which were part of the Corinthians passage but which came before the misquoted lines. Of course it is equally possible that this connection is accidental, and Shakespeare had no intention of linking his own riff on Corinthians with the name of his character. He might simply have invented the speech and named the character subconsciously, as part of his general steeping in the language of the Bible. It could even be a complete coincidence, and since so much of this book argues that "shake" and "spear" turned up accidentally, I must allow this possibility. However, the fact that Bottom then mentions his own name after the misquotation, and even puns on it ("It shall be called Bottom's Dream, because it hath no bottom"), using the same sense of "bottom" which is found in the Biblical text, this seems extremely improbable.

Unlike the Psalm 46 legend, this connection satisfies the tests I have been applying through this first section of the book. It makes sense within the historical context of the writing and performance of the texts in question:

we know that Shakespeare drew on the language of the Bible, and that the people listening to his plays would be capable of hearing the misquotation and mentally making the connection between the two uses of the word "bottom", encouraged by the end of the speech.[36] It fits the textual history of the Bible and the Shakespearean texts: it is a connection with the right version of the Bible for Shakespeare to have heard and absorbed when he was younger. It also fulfils the more nebulous poetic or literary test I have been discussing in this chapter, since it actually adds something to the meaning of the lines. Bottom the awestruck and babbling artisan is connected with the mysterious "bottom" of God's secrets in a pun which teases out some of the ideas we can find in *Midsummer Night's Dream* more generally, such as the truth to be found in confusion, or the interweaving of the noble and supernatural with the homely and the mundane. Putting these two texts side by side does something which the Psalm 46 legend does not, in adding a depth and a nuance to the meaning of the poetic text.

This chapter has built on the historical and textual evidence I discussed earlier, to present an argument which rests on slightly more nebulous and speculative foundations. I have suggested that the Psalm 46 legend is implausible because it fails to make sense of the poetic element in the story, that the psalm as it appears in the King James Bible would not have registered as a "poem" in the same sense as Shakespeare's works, and that there were other poets of the time producing far more literary versions of the psalms. This is a contention partly based on historical fact, since it depends on what we know people in Shakespeare's time knew about the Psalm's status as poetry, and what other poem-shaped psalms or psalm-influence poems were available in that period. It is also partly based on literary judgement; on a feeling that the Psalm 46 text would not have "read" like poetry to contemporary congregations, and that it does not display the kind of quality and artistry which Shakespeare would have wished to sign. With this judgement—which is very open to challenge by others, based on their different appraisal of poetry—I rest my case against the plausibility of the Psalm 46 legend. In the next chapters

I will switch my attention from the period which the legend is about, to the period in which it has been told. I will examine the status of Shakespeare and the King James Bible at crucial points in the late 19th, 20th and early 21st centuries, and consider why the legend arose.

Victorian Origins

In the first part of this book I have examined the evidence for the possibility that Shakespeare was involved in the writing of the King James Bible, or that the translators deliberately hid his name in the text as a tribute to the playwright. As has become clear, I do not believe the evidence remotely supports this idea, which implicitly raises another question. If there is so little basis to this legend, and if it is so easy to discount it by looking at the historical context, why does it continue to be told?

From this chapter onwards I shall be tackling this question, by scrutinising some of the occasions on which it is told. I shall start by thinking about the context in which the legend first appeared in the late 19th century, then pause to examine a slightly different version told by Rudyard Kipling in the 1930s, before continuing on to a Bible commentary produced by a major US publisher in 2014 which repeats the story. In each case I will enquire into what the legend seems to mean for the people telling it, what view of the world it supports, and how it fits in with the ongoing reputation of Shakespeare and the King James Bible.

As far as historians can tell, the Psalm 46 legend appeared in the late 19th century. It first appears in print at the turn of the 20th century, as Hannibal Hamlin notes, calling it "one very peculiar idea that evolved out of the semi-intellectual soup of Victorian writing on Shakespeare and the Bible".[37] He records that "one writer attributes it to an Eton schoolboy, another to the Irish Classicist Yelverton Tyrrell", and that it was put forward in 1910 in *The Flaming Sword*, "the publication of the Koreshan Unity, an American utopian sect" alongside articles on topics such as the secrets of the pyramids and phrenology.[38] The theory moved into more conventional literary magazines during the ensuing years, and was variously debated and debunked over the twentieth century. In 1976 an Assistant Bishop of London, Mark Hodson, presented a theory in *The Times* that the translators had hidden the words as a tribute to Shakespeare, whilst it was also advanced by the Baconian Society as evidence that Shakespeare's works were in fact by the courtier and philosopher Francis Bacon.[39] I have already argued at length that the legend is not true, and this brief sketch of its appearance (if not its origins) tends to reinforce that. Its printing as an esoteric code in *The Flaming Sword* followed by its adoption as a literary curio or a Baconian cipher, suggests it is a coincidence which encourages those who have noticed it to produce narratives based on their own interests, rather than engaging in historical deduction and building hypotheses which fit with all the other evidence we have about the Early Modern theatre and the production of the King James Bible. The narratives which they choose to spin around this coincidence reveal something about what they want to believe about the world. There is a mythic quality to the Psalm 46 legend: it explains a surprising fact in the present by a dramatic tale from the distant past, it provides an origins story for the King James Bible which links it to current values, it replaces the gradual work of lots of people with a single act by a hero, and it makes implicit statements about what we should regard as important. All these push the Psalm 46 narratives away from the category of history and towards that of myth, in the sense of a story which a community tells to explain its situation and assert its values. The fact that these myths centre on Shakespeare and the King James Bible is the result of the particularly high esteem those texts are held in by some parts of English-speaking culture in Britain and the US. To understand this better, we can look at how their reputation stood at the specific moment when these legends started to appear in the late 19th century.

How Shakespeare Became The Bard

During the 19th century Shakespeare was firmly established as an icon of English-speaking culture, and the standard by which all other writers and artists could be compared. Two developments in Shakespeare's reputation are particularly important for our investigation of the Psalm 46 legend, and (perhaps paradoxically) they are connected with the appearance of theories about Shakespeare not having written the plays ascribed to him.[40] To understand why Shakespeare seemed so important that people wanted to believe he had helped write the King James Bible, and why this coincided with conspiracy theories appearing about the authorship of the plays, we need to examine these two strands of how the 19th century imagined him and his reputation.

The first is an increasing focus on biography: Shakespeare became framed as one of the "great men of history" with whom Victorian culture was fascinated. This century saw a number of biographies of Shakespeare, as well as attempts to understand his personality via his works, and an interest in tracing his artistic and personal development through the chronology of the plays. It may not be a coincidence that Victorian literary culture produced some major writers who were also very conscious public figures with larger-than-life personas, such as Charles Dickens, John Ruskin, Walter Pater and Oscar Wilde. With writers like this in the public eye, and the Victorian interest in using history to understand the world around them, Shakespeare the man came under increasing scrutiny during this period. It is telling that when the New Shakespeare Society was founded in 1874, in order to set the study of Shakespeare on a modern and scientific footing, its founder Frederick Furnivall declared its aims to be

> by a very close study of the metrical and phraseological peculiarities of Shakspere [sic], to get his plays as nearly as possible into the order in which he wrote them ... and then to use that revised order for the purpose of studying the progress and meaning of Shakspere's mind [41]

Though the technical and empirical approach of 19th-century science was to be employed, with all the associated ideas of progress and establishing order upon the material world, Furnivall hoped to end with a discovery of the personal life and character of Shakespeare himself. He already had an idea of what that personal life would look like, when it was established by close technical analysis of the plays:

> from the fun and word-play, the lightness, the passion of the Comedies of Youth, through the patriotism (still with comedy of more meaning) of the Histories of Middle Age, to the great Tragedies dealing with the deepest questions of man in Later Life; and then at last to the poet's peaceful and quiet home-life again in Stratford, where he ends with his Prospero and Miranda, his Leontes finding again his wife and daughter in Hermione and Perdita; in whom we may fancy that the Stratford both of his early and late days lives again, and that the daughters he saw there, the sweet English maidens, the pleasant country scenes around him, passt [sic] as it were again into his plays.[42]

This was, after all, one of the great eras of the English novel, so many of which were organised around the development of a central character, whose name might even provide the title of the book, as with *Jane Eyre* or

David Copperfield. We can see Furnivall using Shakespeare's plays, in their various genres, to build a narrative of personal growth and development through his literary career, which is mapped directly onto an imagined personal life.

The second development was the acceleration of Shakespeare's reputation, even beyond the high esteem and status as the national poet which he had achieved in the 18th century, towards the idea of divine inspiration. Through the 19th century, praise of Shakespeare went beyond over-enthusiasm into statements which might sound satirical to modern ears. The praise heaped upon Shakespeare went further than appreciation of his art or even his creative influence, into suggesting that he had an almost mystical and transcendent talent. Carlyle remarked that:

> the best judgement not of this country only, but of Europe at large, is slowly pointing to the conclusion, that Shakespeare is the chief of all Poets hitherto; the greatest intellect who, in our recorded world, has left record of himself in the way of literature.[43]

In even more remarkable phrase, the German poet Henrich Heine declared that "even though God claims for Himself the first place in creation, Shakespeare is next in line", whilst the English writer Thomas Lovell Beddoes wrote in a poem about "the honey-minutes of the year/ Which make man god, and make a god – Shakespeare".[44] Carlyle again expanded on the theme, calling the playwright "a *Prophet*", a "Priest of Mankind" and "a blessed heaven-sent Bringer of Light", whose work could be described (strikingly for our topic) as "a kind of universal Psalm".[45] Shakespeare was being discussed in terms which raised him almost above the human sphere, and framed him as someone who might be in contact with divinity, or might even be comparable to God in some ways. Despite the continuing influence of Shakespeare in our cultural life, it is difficult to imagine modern writers and literary critics describing Shakespeare in terms of divinity (though this may be because public discussion of the arts no longer regards "divine" as the highest praise).

This remarkable attitude to Shakespeare's greatness, combined with the biographical emphasis and interest in the author's life, led to the hypotheses (or conspiracy theories) about Shakespeare not being the author of Shakespeare's plays, according to James Shapiro's *Contested Will*. Put bluntly, a glove-maker's son from Warwickshire could not live up to the hype surrounding Shakespeare, when the same people describing him as semi-divine also wanted to know about his personality and his home life. Surely no-one could have lived up to what was being said about Shakespeare. The Shakespeare of the plays, who was being described as in touch with divinity, didn't entirely fit with the details of Shakespeare's life which the historical sources provided: a young man from a provincial family, with a decent but unspectacular education, who came to London to pursue a career, and made enough money to return to his hometown and buy a big house. Some of the Victorians who wanted to understand the mind of the greatest talent of all time were somewhat disappointed by the small-town boy they found, and some turned to fantasy and conspiracy to explain the discrepancy. There is, as scholars such as Taylor have pointed out, a certain amount of old-fashioned British snobbery involved in a lot of the alternative theories around

Shakespeare's authorship of the plays. Somehow it is never another provincial son of a working-class artisan who turns out to be behind the literary genius: more usually it's a shadowy nobleman with enormous power, or a literary talent who went to university, or even Queen Elizabeth herself. This does suggest that part of the problem is Shakespeare's resolutely unglamorous background, and a desire on the part of some readers for him to have had a more flamboyant and aristocratic life. (Put less charitably, it suggests that some people cannot believe that true genius ever came from the working classes instead of the rich and powerful elites.)

Thus by the time the Psalm 46 legend started appearing, Shakespeare's reputation had risen to such an extent that he was being discussed in barely human terms. To some people he was the transcendent, god-like genius whose character could only be explained by elaborate conspiracy theories instead of the story of a working-class literary talent who made some serious money in London and then retired to spend it. Shakespeare so dominated the Early Modern period, according to this view, that anything of value from that time would inevitably be associated with him. Certainly the King James Bible, the other great cultural monument from the early 17th century, was a prime candidate to be coupled with Shakespeare's name. We might say that by the 20th century many people were waiting for a theory that would link the two icons together: the coincidence of the wording in Psalm 46 didn't start a belief that they were connected, but rather allowed people to indulge their historical fantasies about what "should" have been the case. Shakespeare, the divine poet, and the King James Bible, the divine book, must have been connected, and Psalm 46 provided the pretext around which a story could be spun.

How the King James Bible Became Inspired

I have just referred to the King James Bible as "the divine book", and this points to the other historical trajectory which I believe led to the Psalm 46 legend: the growing veneration of this version in English-speaking culture as not only *an* English Bible but *the* English Bible. The particular connection the Psalm 46 legend makes between Shakespeare and the King James Bible may be read as a result of the latter's history as well as Shakespeare's. David Norton stresses the unusual regard accorded to this particular version of the English Bible in his *History of the English Bible as Literature*, coining the term "AVolatry" for the disproportionate reverence, amounting to worship, directed at the "Authorized Version". (Norton mentions that his term is derived from "bibliolatry", but there is a strong parallel to G.B. Shaw's dismissive term "Bardolatry", demonstrating how intertwined the histories of these two texts are in the 19th and 20th century.)[46] This was not always the case: as I described in the first chapter, the King James Bible developed out of a political situation rather than a purely religious project, and was directed towards tweaking and altering the existing wording rather than totally retranslating the Scriptures. However, after decades of use it came to hold a particular status as the most revered version of the Bible in English.

This took some time, particularly as regards the literary qualities with which many people now credit it. As David Norton has pointed out, many 18th-century readers and critics regarded the King James Bible's style as uncouth, awkward, lacking in eloquence and even "barbarous". The greater appreciation of its language and style in the 19th century was influenced by a number of factors, a few of which are worth noting here, if only speculatively.

Firstly, the passage of time meant that the King James Bible gained authority, with readers and listeners perhaps feeling instinctively that the order of the words was "right" simply because of their long familiarity with this version. The use of the "Authorized Version" every week, and at moments of particular significance such as baptisms, weddings and funerals, could have imbued its words with a level of meaning for many people which was easily confused (or blended) with an appreciation of its literary meaningfulness.

Secondly, literary taste shifted dramatically during the 19th century, so that different qualities came to be regarded as the hallmarks of good style. A number of features of the King James Bible which are often praised today—such as its use of direct language, words of fewer syllables and generally Anglo-Saxon rather than Latinate vocabulary—were generally considered to be literary defects in the 18th century. In contrast, 18th-century taste generally elevated complex constructions, elaborate phrasing, Latin vocabulary and indirect ways of writing: the poetry of Alexander Pope provides a good example. The King James Bible's text could stay exactly the same and be regarded as uncouth and embarrassing in one century, only to be hailed as stylish and vigorous in the next era.

Thirdly it seems likely that the passing of time made the language so out-dated that it became excitingly strange and poetic to the ears of congregations. For 18th-century readers, the phrasing of this version could have sounded close enough to their language that its differences appeared to be faults and mistakes: it sounded like an attempt to write in contemporary English but with old-fashioned vocabulary and out-dated ways of using language. After another 100 years, the King James Bible's language would have sounded even further away from the language of everyday life and of literary compositions, and this might paradoxically have improved its standing in the opinion of readers. In being so far away from "normal" usage it might have stopped sounding old-fashioned and uncultured, and instead sounded archaic and elevated. It could have sounded less like a failed attempt to render ideas in modern English, and more like another language entirely, with its own dignity and style.

Whatever the causes, the 19th century saw a significant rise in the value accorded to the King James Bible. The appreciation of Hartley Coleridge in 1833 goes as far as implying that the King James Bible is the result of English in its prelapsarian state, before a "Fall" comparable to that which takes place in Genesis:

> We doubt, indeed, whether any new translation, however learned, exact or truly orthodox, will ever appear to English Christians to be the real Bible. The language of the Authorized Version is the perfection of English, and it can never be written again, for the language of prose is one of the few things in which the English have really degenerated. Our tongue has lost its holiness. [47]

This argument is couched in relatively practical terms, proposing only that the King James Bible will "appear" to always be the "real Bible", not that it necessarily has some unique spiritual characteristics, and that its unrepeatable quality is due to the time in which it was written, when English prose was much better. Nonetheless, though Coleridge takes an apparently pragmatic approach, the result is that the King James Bible is the definitive English version of the Bible, which is not only better than the other attempts which have been made, but also better than any which ever could be made in the future. The "degeneration" of English prose he identifies means that English-speaking readers will have to be content with the King James Bible and never hope to ever see a revision or retranslation which could improve on it. There is even a touch of the supernatural in the poetic phrase about the English "tongue" having "lost its holiness", which dimly recalls the curses which the Psalmist calls down upon themselves in Babylon: "If I forget thee, O Jerusalem, let my right hand forget her cunning … let my tongue cleave to the roof of my mouth".

This supernatural—or spiritual—aspect of the King James Bible's quality was much more enthusiastically argued by other, more extreme, proponents of the translation. In 1857, the American evangelist Alexander McClure published a biographical account of the translators of the King James Bible. McClure's discussion begins, like Coleridge's, with historical elements, but moves with greater abandon into the realm of religion and divine influence.

> The first half of the seventeenth century, when the translation was completed, was the *Golden Age* of biblical and oriental learning in England. Never before, nor since, have these studies been pursued by scholars whose vernacular tongue is the English with such zeal and industry and success. This remarkable fact is a token of God's providential care of his word as deserves most devout acknowledgment.[48]

The practical and historical issues of the translation, such as the context of the work and the general state of knowledge about ancient languages, is not simply advanced as a reason for the excellence of the King James Bible, but as proof that something else is going on behind the scenes. Having declared that the period was a "Golden Age" for this kind of work, McClure deduces that this situation was itself the result of "God's providential care of his word". In a startling twist of logic, a supernatural cause is deduced from the very natural causes which other scholars might take to prove that no supernatural cause was necessary.

McClure develops his idea in more detail:

> ...But we hold that the translators enjoyed the highest degree of that special guidance which is ever granted to God's true servants in exigencies of deep concernment to his kingdom on earth. Such special succors and spiritual assistances are always vouchsafed where there is a like union of piety, of prayers and of pains to effect an object of such incalculable importance to the church of the living God. The necessity of a supernatural revelation to man of the divine will has often been argued in favour of the extreme probability that such a revelation has been made. A like necessity, and one nearly as pressing, might be argued in favour of the belief that this most important of all the versions of God's revealed will must have been made under His peculiar guidance, and His provident eye. And the manner in which that version has met the wants of the most free and intelligent nations in the old world and the new may well confirm us in the persuasion that the same illuminating Spirit which indited the original Scriptures was imparted in such grace to aid and guard the preparation of the English version.[49]

In one sense, this is a relatively modest claim: many modern Christians would emphasise the Holy Spirit's role in the life of any church, and it has been particularly associated in the Christian tradition with the practice of Bible reading. Saying that the same Spirit which helped the original writers also helped the translators might be only saying that they were devout Christians who were carrying out an authentically Christian activity. However, the fact that McClure makes this argument in the context of extolling the particular virtues of this one version of the Bible makes the statement here far more dramatic. He appears to be arguing that the Bible was somehow "re-inspired" during the process of translating the King James Bible, and that there are two specific moments in which the Holy Spirit was present.

McClure is an extreme example of what Norton calls "AVolatry", but this is more due to his theological arguments for the unique quality of the text than his belief in those qualities. Not many other people have argued that the Holy Spirit intervened in history to "re-inspire" the King James Bible, and thus produce an English Bible which was as definitive in its spiritual power as the works of the original authors of the Bible, but many more people have acted as if they thought something similar. McClure might be regarded as unusual partly because he felt the need to make a coherent (if extraordinary) argument about precisely *why* the King James Bible was absolutely the best, and to account for this supposed fact in both historical and theological terms, rather than simply using it, praising it, and treating it as if it were synonymous with God's word.

Shakespeare and the King James Bible Collide

The two historical arcs I have been sketching above—Shakespeare's rise in reputation from a talented playwright to a near-divine genius, and the King James Bible's shift from being regarded as a slightly uncouth translation to the exclusive word of God in English—intersect in the late 19th century with the appearance of the Psalm 46 legend. This was not inevitable, and I am not suggesting that the appearance of such a story could have been deduced from their parallel situations. Nonetheless examining the histories of Shakespeare and the King James Bible over the preceding centuries makes sense of the fact that the legend appears to have arisen in the late 19th century, when their reputations took this particular form.

It was at this moment that it seemed most natural and inevitable to many of the British and US public that there was an immediate and personal connection between William Shakespeare and the King James Bible. Many of them would have studied the plays at school (as modern schoolchildren do), attended performances of them at the theatre and heard the King James Bible read out regularly at church services. Reinforcing and structuring that personal experience was a whole set of institutions, including the theatres and churches, which held up Shakespeare and the (King James) Bible as the pinnacles of English-speaking culture. That influence also pervaded the culture of the time in a less dramatic way: it is striking when reading 19th-century novels and newspapers just how automatically they assume that most readers will recognise references to Shakespeare and the King James Bible. A few examples of this will give a sense of the pervading presence of these texts for readers and writers across the era.

Thomas Hughes' influential novel *Tom Brown's School Days* was published in the late 1850s, and displays a series of references to Shakespeare and the Bible. This is perhaps not surprising in an explicitly didactic novel intended to instruct and improve its readers, and to include a quantity of what Hughes himself acknowledged as "preaching". The descriptions of school life are frequently overlaid by references which call attention to the greater importance of what is taking place, and emphasise the moral dimension of the story. For example, the appearance of the School Captain, "old Brooke", in a game of rugby:

> and old Brooke ranges the field like Job's war-horse. The thickest scrummage parts asunder before his rush, like the waves before a clipper's bows; his cheery voice rings out over the field, and his eye is everywhere.[50]

The mention of Job is intended to call up the description of the horse from the Book of Job (in the King James Bible here):

> He paweth in the valley, and rejoiceth in his strength: he goeth on to meet the armed men. He mocketh at fear, and is not affrighted; neither turneth he back from the sword. The quiver rattleth against him, the glittering spear and the shield. He swalloweth the ground with fierceness and rage: neither believeth he that it is the sound

> of the trumpet. He saith among the trumpets, Ha, ha; and he smelleth the battle afar off, the thunder of the captains, and the shouting.

Hughes' reference swathes the rugby captain in this paean to power and fearlessness, giving greater stature to the events happening on the page, and insisting that schoolboys are capable of displaying the virtues to be found in the Biblical texts. (The combination of Job's war-horse and a clipper's bows in the imagery suggests a particularly Victorian blend of Biblical precedent and imperial ambition being commended to the readers.) Hughes obviously had a special place for this passage in his imagination, as it appears less explicitly at two other crucial points. When he describes the country fair, with its rough and ready games, he laments what he sees as the decay of similar English customs, and the tendency of the squires to seek entertainment in London rather than supporting village ways:

> Only I have just got this to say before I quit the text. Don't let reformers of any sort think that they are going really to lay hold of the working boys and young men of England by any educational grapnel whatever, which isn't some bon fide equivalent for the games of the old country "veast" [feast] in it; something to put in

> place of the back-swording and wrestling and racing; something to try the muscles of men's bodies, and the endurance of their hearts, and to make them rejoice in their strength. In all the new-fangled comprehensive plans which I see, this is all left out, and the consequence is, that your great mechanics' institutes end in intellectual priggism, and your Christian young men's societies in religious Pharisaism.[51]

The strenuous games which are necessary for young men's development will make them "rejoice in their strength": the war-horse isn't explicitly mentioned, but there is a definite echo here. Likewise when Hughes describes the first time Tom hears the headmaster preach in chapel:

> the long lines of young faces, rising tier above tier down the whole length of the chapel, from the little boy's who had just left his mother to the young man's who was going out next week into the great world, rejoicing in his strength. It was a great and solemn sight.[52]

This quotation connects together moments in which Hughes presents his sense of what boys and young men should be like. Whether it was deliberately designed by him to link the sermons, the game of rugby and the games at the fair with the horse in Job, or whether he was simply so familiar with the language of the Bible that he used the phrase when it came to hand, is not clear. Likewise some readers may have recognised the quotation as a reference back to Job, and others simply appreciated it as a resonant and vaguely Biblical-sounding phrase. In another portion of the book, Hughes brings Shakespeare and the Bible into the same narrative episode. Tom and his friend East, still in the lower years, have led a small rebellion in the school against the unfair treatment of the younger boys by some bullies in the fifth form. When the head bully, named Flashman, is expelled, the older boys still regard Tom and East with some suspicion, even though their rebellion was justified. Hughes remarks:

> The evil that men and boys too do lives after them: Flashman was gone, but our boys, as hinted above, still felt the effects of his fate … The cause was righteous – the result had been triumphant to a great extent; but the best of the fifth … couldn't help feeling a small grudge against the first rebels.[53]

This is a quotation from one of the most famous speeches in Shakespeare's works: Mark Antony's funeral oration in *Julius Caesar*:

> Friends, Roman, countrymen, lend me your ears!
> I come to bury Caesar, not to praise him.
> The evil that men do lives after them,
> The good is oft interred with their bones;
> So let it be with Caesar.[54]

The multiple layers of irony going on this speech do not make themselves felt in Hughes' reference, but it is more than just a detached quotation about the after-effects of evil. Tom and East have slain a tyrant by standing up to Flashman, but the after-effects are still continuing.

In the same (lengthy) passage, Hughes comments that "East and Tom, the Tadpole, and one or two more, became a sort of young Ishmaelites, their hands against every one, and every one's hands against them". The Ishmaelites are a tribe in Genesis, who appear in various stories, most notoriously buying Joseph from his brothers to sell him into slavery in Egypt. This comment, however, is a reference to the figure whom from the tribe took its name: Ishmael, Abram's son by his slave Hagar:

> And the angel of the LORD said unto her [Hagar], Behold, thou art with child and shalt bear a son, and shalt call his name Ishmael; because the LORD hath heard thy affliction. And he will be a wild man; his hand will be against every man, and every man's hand against him; and he shall dwell in the presence of all his brethren.[55]

The precise verbal reference here connects Tom and East (and the other rebels) to Ishmael, highlighting the fact that they were at enmity with the people they lived around, and were "wild men" outside the community's customs, despite their justified actions. As with Job's horse, the links Hughes makes here with Ishmael and *Julius Caesar* provide parallel narratives, suggesting that apparently trivial episodes in a school involve the same kinds of moral and political issues as their much more famous equivalents. This is a central part of Hughes' message in the book, which is concerned to recommend a muscular Christianity to boys and young men, and to assure them that every day is a moral struggle in which they need to display the characteristics of Biblical and Shakespearean heroes.

Rather more light-hearted references to these texts can be found in Anthony Trollope's work, though he also took his fictional worlds seriously. An explicit reference to Shakespeare, though not by name, comes in his comic novel *The Struggles of Brown, Jones and Robinson*. The narrator, a keen young businessman without any capital, is arguing the value of modern trade methods and hyperbolic advertisements over the more staid approach of old-fashioned firms:

> There are those – men of the old school ... who say that advertisements do not keep the promises which they make. But what says the poet, – he whom we teach our children to read? What says the stern moralist to his wicked mother in the play? "Assume a virtue if you have it not" and so say I. "Assume a virtue if you have it not." It would be a great trade virtue in the haberdasher to have forty thousand pairs of best hose lying ready for sale in his warehouse. Let him assume that virtue if he have it not."[56]

Here Trollope signals that this is a quotation from literature, and gives a hint as to the origin of it by mentioning a play and a wicked mother. However, the joke depends on a significant quantity of knowledge in the reader to work properly: it assumes that the reader will recognise the play as *Hamlet* (either from the line or from the description of the situation) and know that this is a complete misapplication of Hamlet's words to Gertrude. The injunction to "assume a virtue if you have it not", i.e. to behave morally even if that does not accord with her inner feelings, is turned round to suggest that tradesmen should advertise goods for sale which they do not actually possess.

Quotation and business methods come into connection again in another of Trollope's novels, when a young man who has inherited a share of a brewery is trying to persuade the brewer to make changes in the firm, and invest in new machinery, much against the older man's inclination:

> "I don't know about that. I certainly want to improve the concern."
>
> "Ah, yes; and so ruin it. Whereas I've been making money out of it these thirty years. You and I won't do together; that's the long of it and the short of it."
>
> "It would be a putting of new wine into old bottles, you think?" suggested Rowan.
>
> "I'm not saying anything about wine; but I do think that I ought to know something about beer."[57]

The character named Rowan here is making a reference to Jesus' words in the Gospels:

> No man putteth a piece of new cloth unto an old garment, for that which is put in to fill it up taketh from the garment, and the rent is made worse. Neither do men put new wine into old bottles: else the bottles break and the wine runneth out, and the bottles perish: but they put new wine into new bottles, and both are preserved.[58]

Of course, Jesus' words are intended as a metaphor, as the passage before about the cloth makes clear. They are part of the Messianic and apocalyptic strain in the Gospels, emphasising the radically new implications of Jesus' life and teachings when compared to the existing order of things. Rowan is using them in the same sense, suggesting that the older man thinks his new ideas for innovations will simply not be possible in the business as it stands. The older man apparently takes his metaphor literally, and insists that he doesn't know anything about wine, since beer is his business. As with the *Hamlet* reference above, the humour of this passage depends upon the reader recognising the quotation, and appreciating how it is being misunderstood in the novel. In this case, a reader who appreciates the distance between Jesus' words and the brewer's focus on beer, is subtly placed on the side of Rowan, the younger man. They share a knowledge which the other character in the scene does not possess, implicitly directing the reader's sympathies. The reference both demonstrates the character of the two men—the one more concerned with metaphors and new possibilities, the other more concerned with immediate and physical things—and develops an understanding between the writer and the reader.

Trollope and his readers were so steeped in the language of Shakespeare and the King James Bible that the two texts sometimes overlap in the same passage, as in this description of an austerely religious lady looking at the decaying street she lived in:

> For Mrs. Winterfield herself this desolation had, I think, a certain melancholy attraction. It suited her mind and her religious views that she should be thus daily reminded that things of this world were passing away and going to destruction. She liked to have ocular proof that grass was growing in the highways under mortal feet, and that it was no longer worth man's while to renew human flags in human streets.[59]

The passage is jokily redolent with the phraseology of the King James Bible. It echoes Paul's declaration in 1 Corinthians 7:31 that "the fashion of this world passeth away" and the vision of Revelation 21:4 that "the former things are passed away". "Highways" is not an unusual word, but in the context of Mrs. Winterfield's thoughts it might recall Amos 5:16, "Wailing shall be in all streets, and they shall say in all the highways, Alas! alas!" The image of grass next to things passing away and destruction calls up Psalm 90's meditation on human frailty:

> thou turnest man to destruction ... in the morning they are like grass which groweth up. In the morning it flourisheth, and groweth up; in the evening it is cut down, and withereth ... For all our days are passed away in thy wrath.

This is not so much a reference to a particular story or verse, as much as a rhapsody of certain phrases which express themes of destruction and judgement in the King James Bible. In amongst them appears the phrase "ocular proof", which Trollope has borrowed from Shakespeare. In his fury at the suggestion that Desdemona has been unfaithful to him, Othello demands of Iago "Be sure of it. Give me the ocular proof".[60] To the reader alert to the quotation's source, this potentially undermines the whole of Mrs. Winterfield's mediation. The sin that Othello demands "ocular proof" of has not actually taken place, and the play's plot hinges on a clue—the handkerchief—which Othello believes is reliable "ocular proof" but is nothing of the kind. Amidst the doom-laden (if slightly self-satisfied) reflections of the religious character, a phrase appears which comes from a very different source, and which famously suggests that people may drastically misinterpret things which are in front of their very eyes.

At the turn of the 20th century many novelists could still rely on a knowledge of the King James Bible and Shakespeare in their readers. One of P.G. Wodehouse's first books, *The Gold Bat*, was published in 1904 and demonstrates a similar assumption of Biblical and Shakespearean literacy, combined with an ironic and even flippant tone. In describing a school sports competition, the narrator states:

> There were twelve houses at Wrykyn, and they played on the 'knocking-out' system. To be beaten once meant that a house was no longer eligible for the competition. It could play 'friendlies' as much as it liked, but, play it never so wisely, it could not lift the cup.[61]

The slightly odd construction "play it never so wisely" is a reference to Psalm 58 in the King James Bible, "they are like the deaf adder that stoppeth her ear; Which will not hearken to the voice of charmers, charming never so wisely". At another point in the story a schoolboy with literary tastes is puzzling over how to find a quiet place in the rowdy school to enjoy a quiet read. He decides to read after lights out in his study:

> Why, he thought, should he not go and read in his study with a dark lantern? He had a dark lantern. It was one of the things he had found lying about at home on the last day of the holidays, and had brought with him to school. It was his custom to go about the house just before the holidays ended, snapping up unconsidered trifles, which might or might not come in useful.[62]

This description of his habit of pilfering whatever he found lying around at home includes a recognisable echo of the thieving Autolycus in *The Winter's Tale*: "My father nam'd me Autolycus, who being, as I am, litter'd under Mercury, was likewise a snapper-up of unconsider'd trifles". In a rather longer passage, also concerned with winning sports trophies, Wodehouse packs in a number of verbal echoes. The previous school cup has been replaced by a newer and more impressive one:

> The question now arose: what was to be done with the other cup? The School House, who happened to be the holders at the time, suggested disinterestedly that it should become the property of the house which had won it last. "Not so", replied the Field Sports Committee, "but far otherwise. We will have it melted down in a fiery furnace, and thereafter fashioned into eleven little silver bats. And these little silver bats shall be the guerdon of the eleven members of the winning team, to have and to hold for the space of one year, unless, by winning the cup twice in succession, they gain the right of keeping the bat for yet another year. How is that, umpire?" And the authorities replied "O men of infinite resource and sagacity, verily it is a cold day when *you* get left behind. Forge ahead." But, when they had forged ahead, behold! it would not run to eleven little silver bats, but only to ten little silver bats. Thereupon the headmaster, a man liberal with his cash, caused an eleventh little bat to be fashioned – for the captain of the winning team to have and to hold in the manner aforesaid. And, to single it out from the others, it was wrought,

> not of silver, but of gold. And so it came to pass that at the time of our story Trevor was in possession of the little gold bat.[63]

This is a tour de force of pastiche, parody and quotation, and there are some elements in it which do not lead back to either Shakespeare or the King James Bible. "Not so, but far otherwise", for example, is borrowed from Rudyard Kipling's *Just So Stories*, as is "infinite resource and sagacity", whilst "to have and to hold" is taken from the wedding service in the Book of Common Prayer. The formula "How is that, umpire?" used to end the committee's suggestion is the formal cry of a cricketer claiming a wicket and asking for a decision from the umpire (though it is more frequently heard as "Howzaaaat?!"), whilst "in the manner aforesaid" is a pastiche of legal phraseology.

With those phrases noted, the passage as a whole is heavily influenced by the King James Bible. There are individual phrases borrowed directly from the Bible, but which do not reference a specific passage: "it came to pass" is one of the building blocks of Biblical narrative, appearing more than 450 times in the King James Bible, and "behold" is used over 500 times, whilst "space of" to refer to time has only 16 appearances, but is still clearly Biblical. These phrases give the passage as a whole the air of a pastiche of Biblical narratives, as does the use of lengthy phrases repeated in full, in "into eleven little silver bats. And these eleven little silver bats" and "would not run to eleven little silver bats, but only to ten little silver bats". This technique is typical of ancient narratives such as Genesis and the works of Homer, which have their origins in oral storytelling. It's much rarer in written narratives, and is noticeable here because of its difference from Wodehouse's usual style. Like the use of "came to pass", it does not invoke a specific passage, but Pharaoh's dream in Genesis provides an example:

> And it came to pass at the end of two full years that Pharaoh dreamed: and, behold, he stood by the river. And, behold, there came up out of the river seven well favoured kine and fatfleshed; and they fed in a meadow. And, behold, seven other kine came up after them out of the river, ill favoured and leanfleshed; and stood by the other kind upon the brink of the river. And the ill favoured and leanfleshed kine did eat up the seven well favoured and fat kine. So Pharaoh awoke.[64]

The repetitive structure gives a particular weight and feel to the passage, which Wodehouse replicates in his jocular anecdote. There are also phrases which recall episodes in the King James Bible more specifically. "Fiery furnace" is used only in the story of Daniel and his companions who were ordered to worship a golden idol by Nebuchadnezzar, on pain of being cast into a fiery furnace. The theme of idols made from melted metals is paralleled in the idol made by the Israelites whilst Moses was on Mount Sinai:

> And all the people brake off their golden earrings which were in their ears, and brought them unto Aaron. And he received them at their hand, and fashioned it with a graving tool, after he had made it a molten calf: and they said, These be thy gods, O Israel.[65]

Both Aaron and the committee have precious metal melted and "fashioned" into a valuable object, setting up a comic echo of this serious story in the creation of the prizes for which the cricket teams compete.

The word "guerdon" is an archaic term for a reward, but it has a particular significance in one of Shakespeare's plays which makes me interpret this as a verbal echo rather than simply an old-fashioned word. In *Love's Labour's Lost*, the clown Costard is given money by two characters for running errands for them, Don Armado, who calls it his "remuneration", and Biron, who calls it a "guerdon". These lines result:

> BIRON: ... [giving him a letter and money] There's thy guerdon. Go.
>
> COSTARD: Guerdon! O sweet guerdon! Better than remuneration, elevenpence-farthing better. Most sweet guerdon! I will do it, sir, in print. Guerdon – remuneration![66]

The relatively simple joke here—that Costard thinks "remuneration" and "guerdon" are the names of coins rather than elaborate ways of saying "here's your money"—is an ongoing gag in the play. Wodehouse's use of the obscure word is most likely to have been prompted by the playing on it in Shakespeare's comedy. Wodehouse's verbal dexterity contains both a plethora of references to Shakespeare and the Bible, and a knowing mesh of irony and comedy in his weaving of them together alongside other literary sources.

These three novelists demonstrate some of the ways in which the language of Shakespeare's plays and the King James Bible pervaded literature of this period. I could have chosen other writers, but I thought these three showed a variety of kinds of engagement, and—more importantly—showed these texts being cited in popular works intended for the general reader. Hughes, Trollope and Wodehouse were not abstruse or highbrow authors, they wrote very successful works for a broad readership. Thus their engagement with the canonical texts under discussion goes some way to showing the kind of knowledge they could assume in their audience. As I pointed out, the citations and references are more than verbal flourishes, and are often essential to the meaning of the passage, particularly in the comic passages.

I have suggested above that the Psalm 46 legend takes advantage of a coincidence to weave a story about something which many people feel ought to have happened. In hindsight the point at which the legend appeared in print, and in public discussion, was very likely the moment at which that feeling was most strong. Viewed from this angle, the legend is not a theory about the relationship between the works of Shakespeare and the text of the King James Bible, but neither is it a completely random and nonsensical fable for which there is no explanation.

Rather, it is a revealing episode in the parallel histories of these two collections of texts, which shows those histories intersecting in a bizarre but comprehensible way. In the next chapter, I will pause for a moment in the analysis of the Psalm 46 legend, in order to examine another story in which Shakespeare had a hand in the wording of the King James Bible. Rudyard Kipling's short story "Proofs of Holy Writ" imagines an episode in which Shakespeare and Ben Jonson collaborated with the official translators on a passage of the prophet Isaiah. The appearance of another tale of this type, but which concentrates on a different passage of the Bible, suggests that the argument of this chapter has some merit, and that the connection between the playwright and the King James Bible had a powerful appeal to the imagination of the time.

Kipling's Daemon

This chapter is an interlude in the discussion of the Psalm 46 legend, to consider another story about Shakespeare's involvement with the King James Bible. Rudyard Kipling is famous as a 19th-century man of letters, a poet of Empire and an author of children's stories, but at the end of his life he wrote a short story about Shakespeare and the translation of the King James Bible. "Proofs of Holy Writ" does not mention Psalm 46, but rather Isaiah, and the story is prefaced by these lines:

1. ARISE, shine: for thy light is come, and the glory of the Lord is risen upon thee.
2. For, behold, the darkness shall cover the earth, and gross darkness the people: but the Lord shall arise upon thee, and his glory shall be seen upon thee.
3. And the Gentiles shall come to thy light, and kings to the brightness of thy rising.
    ...
19. The sun shall be no more thy light by day; neither for brightness shall the moon give light unto thee: but the Lord shall be unto thee an everlasting light, and thy God thy glory.
20. Thy sun shall no more go down; neither shall thy moon withdraw itself: for the Lord shall be thine everlasting light, and the days of thy mourning shall be ended.

The story is included as an appendix at the end of this book: I will quote and paraphrase parts of it below, but it is well worth a read, especially to get a sense of the tone and style. The story is set in the early years of the 17th century, when two men are sitting in a summerhouse bickering good-naturedly about the plays they've written and the other authors they've quarrelled with. The reader soon realises that the two characters are William Shakespeare and Ben Jonson. Kipling's approach is dense and allusive, and he presents the two literary friends picking up familiar ideas and arguments in their conversations without spelling them out in exposition into the reader. Jonson's duel with Gabriel Spencer, and the literary quarrel known as the Poetomachia or War of the Theatres are just two of the literary-historical topics to which the two characters refer obliquely, and the different English versions of the Bible are similarly dropped into the conversation without comment. In doing this, the story offers a richly-textured imaginary scene, inviting readers into a literary dream about what it might have been like to hear Shakespeare and Jonson chatting about their lives and writings, but it also sets up a set of small puzzles and challenges. The reader needs a certain amount of literary and historical knowledge to understand the references the characters make (though it is enjoyable even without that knowledge), and is encouraged to decode the oblique comments, alert for meanings hidden below the surface.

When considering the narrative's engagement with Shakespeare and the King James Bible, perhaps the first clue to the meaning of this story—or a suggestion about how we might interpret it—is in the title. "Holy Writ" is a general phrase used to refer to sacred scriptures, but "Proofs of Holy Writ" is a quotation of a line from *Othello*. In the context of the play, Iago has acquired Desdemona's handkerchief, and plans to plant it somewhere which will make Othello think Desdemona has been unfaithful to him. He says:

> I will in Cassio's lodging lose this napkin
> And let him find it. Trifles light as air
> Are to the jealous confirmations strong
> As proofs of holy writ. This may do something.
> The Moor already changes with my poison. [67]

Aside from making a connection between the title and one of the characters by quoting Shakespeare, Kipling's title might contain a hint about his attitude to the legend. In its original context it is a line about how gullible people are, and how they will entirely over-read any trace of evidence which convinces them of something they already intend to believe. People want to find a connection between Shakespeare and the King James Bible, it suggests, and therefore they will seize on any trifling coincidence in order to claim the connection has been proved. There's an irony here, of course, as Iago is commenting on the difference between "trifles light as air" and "proofs of holy writ", when the trifle in question is actually part of holy writ. Having said that, this interpretation of the title depends upon a close scrutiny of the quotation and its meaning in the original play. Perhaps it is a joke about people who try to work out the entire meaning of the story from an apparently throwaway quotation in the title; perhaps the *Othello* quotation is the "trifl[e] light as air", and the reader who thinks they have discovered Kipling's scorn for the legend has been too quick to find "confirmation" of their prior opinion. The title seems to provide possible traps both for those who believe the legend, and those who don't. Whatever its precise meaning—and its meaning may deliberately involve not being pinned down precisely—it is clear that the quotation from *Othello* encourages readers to think about the story in terms of suspicion, over-interpretation and hidden meanings controlled by other people. Having obligingly over-scrutinised the title, we can consider the actual content of the narrative.

As to the two friends are talking in the garden of Shakespeare's house, a letter arrives by a rider, which turns out to be from one of the translators of the King James Bible:

> 'From the most learned divine, Miles Smith of Brazen Nose College,' Will explained. 'You know this business as well as I. The King has set all the scholars of England to make one Bible, which the Church shall be bound to, out of all the Bibles that men use.'
>
> 'I knew.' Ben could not lift his eyes from the printed page. 'I'm more about Court than you think. The learning of Oxford and Cambridge—"most noble and most equal," as I have said—and Westminster, to sit upon a clutch of Bibles. Those 'ud be Geneva (my mother read to me out of it at her knee), Douai, Rheims, Coverdale, Matthew's, the Bishops', the Great, and so forth.'

Shakespeare explains that Miles Smith was impressed by hearing a performance by one of his plays, in which Richard Burbage starred:

> 'He was moved, he said, with some lines of mine in Dick's part. He said they were, to his godly apprehension, a parable, as it might be, of his reverend self, going down darkling to his tomb 'twixt cliffs of ice and iron.'
>
> 'What lines? I know none of thine of that power. But in my *Sejanus*—'
>
> 'These were in my *Macbeth*. They lost nothing at Dick's mouth:
>
>> '"To-morrow, and tomorrow, and to-morrow
>> Creeps in this petty pace from day to day
>> To the last syllable of recorded time,
>> And all our yesterdays have lighted fools
>> The way to dusty death—"'

Having noticed the brilliance and profundity of Shakespeare's poetry, Smith has written to him to ask his help over a passage of Isaiah which has been giving his group of translators trouble. The rest of the story shows the two poets working through the lines, discussing the meaning of particular words, the correct way to render them into English metre, the Classical and Biblical implications of lines, and the previous English translations. For example:

> "'*Et complebuntur dies luctus tui.*'" Ben read. "'And thy sorrowful days shall be rewarded thee,' says Coverdale.'
>
> 'And the Bishops?'
>
> "'And thy sorrowful days shall be ended.'"
>
> 'By no means. And Douai?'
>
> "'Thy sorrow shall be ended.'"
>
> 'And Geneva?'
>
> "'And the days of thy mourning shall be ended.'"
>
> 'The Switzers have it! Lay the tail of Geneva to the head of Coverdale and the last is without flaw.'

This passage shows what almost no versions of the Psalm 46 legend show: an awareness of the slow textual work which went into the King James Bible, and the multiple existing versions which influenced the precise form of words. It is tempting to see Kipling's experiences as an editor and journalist in this difference, as he depicts the two playwrights taking on a serious commission and marshalling the sources before hashing out the wording that would be most suitable. There is an element of poetic inspiration in the story, nonetheless, as at one point Shakespeare walks away from his companion:

> 'They'll be all there.' Ben referred to the proofs. "'Tis "arise" in both,' said he. '"Arise and be bright" in Geneva. In the Douai 'tis "Arise and be illuminated."'
>
> 'So? Give me the paper now.' Will took it from his companion, rose, and paced towards a tree in the orchard, turning again, when he had reached it, by a well-worn track through the grass. Ben leaned forward in his chair. The other's free hand went up warningly. 'Quiet, man!' said he. 'I wait on my Demon!' He fell into the stage-stride of his art at that time, speaking to the air.

Near the end of the story he rejoices with the words "'We have it! ... Blessed be my Demon!'" Shakespeare's mysterious "demon" is apparently connected with Kipling's own literary inspiration: in his autobiographical writings he talks about "my Daemon" as giving him ideas or telling him to avoid particular things.

> My Daemon was with me in the *Jungle Book, Kim* and both Puck books, and good care I took to walk delicately, lest he should withdraw. I know

> that he did not, because when those books were finished, they said so themselves with, almost, the water-hammer click of a tap turned off. One of the clauses in our contract was that I should never follow up 'a success,' for by this sin fell Napoleon and a few others. *Note here.* When your Daemon is in charge, do not try to think consciously. Drift, wait, and obey.[68]

The idea that a demon (or "daemon", or "daimon") was a supernatural presence, a personal spirit which could be a source of inspiration, appears in Classical literature and philosophy, including the works of Homer and Plato, and Kipling himself mentions "the Personal Daemon of Aristotle and others". I will consider the "Puck books" which the "daemon" helped him to write below, but for the moment it is enough to notice that Kipling embeds his own idea of inspiration in the story of Shakespeare and the Bible. It is both an ancient and a very practical notion, stemming from Classical Greece but capable of telling him to avoid publishing a specific story, or to imagine the background to a tale in a specific way. Given the subject of "Proofs of Holy Writ", it is amusing (and perhaps telling) that Kipling's description of his "contract", as recorded in his memoirs, contains an implied quotation from

Shakespeare. The slightly archaic creak of the phrase "for by this sin fell" signals that he is riffing on Cardinal Wolsey's speech in the lesser-known play *Henry VIII, or, All Is True*:

> Cromwell, I charge thee: fling away ambition:
> By that sin fell the angels; how can man, then,
> The image of his Maker, win by it?[69]

The principle of not trying to capitalise too far on a successful work is raised to almost a deal with an angel by this echo of Wolsey, again demonstrating Kipling's dramatic but professional sense of how his writing worked. This is the kind of inspiration which appears in "Proofs of Holy Writ": a genuinely odd and even magical presence, but one which takes place within the rigorous business of professional writing.

The situation in which the translation takes place might have an echo of the story's origin, which was also that of a meeting of professional writers. In a note to the reprinting of the story in *The Strand* magazine in 1947, it is recorded that the idea for the story arose from a lunch in Fleet Street where the novelist John Buchan and Kipling were discussing the literary qualities of the King James Bible.

> Buchan commented that "it was strange that such splendour had been produced by a body of men learned, no doubt, in theology and in languages, but including among them no writer." Could it be, he wondered, that they had privately consulted the great writers of the age, Shakespeare, perhaps and Jonson and others? Kipling replied "that's an idea", and later consulted George Saintsbury, the Professor of Rhetoric and English Literature at Edinburgh, in working out the details of the story.

It could be a coincidence that the conversation about the literary splendours of the King James Bible which began over a convivial table between two professional writers mulling over the technical aspects of their craft gave rise a story which suggested that those literary splendours were the result of two professional writers mulling over the technical aspects of their craft at a convivial table three centuries previously. It certainly underlines the kind of narrative which "Proofs of Holy Writ" presents about Shakespeare's involvement, and the kind of inspiration and professionalism which it provides as an explanation for the King James Bible's greatness.

It is also worth noting that Buchan's speculation assumed that if the translators had consulted a professional writer, they would have chosen a number of them rather than relying on the genius of Shakespeare as the pre-eminent author of the period. This again locates the version of the legend produced by Kipling in the activities of a recognisable group of literary workers who wrote as a livelihood and had a particular range of skills.

This identification of the Early Modern literary world with the general outlines of writing and publishing in the early 20th century—if only in a speculative conversation over lunch—also obscures one possible answer to Buchan's ponderings. As far as we know (and as far as the evidence shows) no professional writers of poetry or fiction were involved in the production of the King James Bible, but that does not mean that theology and languages were the only areas in which people involved in the project excelled. Preaching was one of the major modes of literary and dramatic expression in the reign of King James, and the Londoner who wanted to while away an afternoon might choose between a play, a bear-baiting and a popular preacher for their entertainment. The eloquence and vigour of sermons was one of the ways in which a churchman might hope to attract the attention of both the people listening to him and the notice of those more senior in the church hierarchy. A great preacher could gather crowds at recognised public places like St. Paul's Cross, or might even be invited to preach before the monarch at Court. James particularly appreciated fine sermons, driven by the keen interest in theology and church politics which led him to convene the Hampton Court conference, and order the translation of the Bible. It was certainly possible to be a priest without the skill of eloquent preaching (as sources from all periods of the Church of England's history attest), but the sermon was a much more recognised form of "literary" expression than it is in our culture. Just as it is difficult (or even meaningless) to try to disentangle religion and politics in the Early Modern world, since these were not recognised as separate spheres in the way they are today, it is difficult to prise religion and art away from each other. The 19th-century notion of "art for art's sake", with its valorisation of the entirely aesthetic realm, deliberately divorced from social purpose or ideological intention, may obscure the literary qualities of sermons and prayers. Perhaps the most famous examples of Jacobean preachers are John Donne and Lancelot Andrewes, whose very different styles both show a high level of conscious artistry. Donne's sermons are more obviously dramatic and intense, as with this description of his difficulties in praying:

> I throw myself down in my chamber, and I call in, and invite God, and his Angels thither, and when they are there, I neglect God and his angels for the noise of a fly, for the rattling of a coach, for the whining of a door; I talk on in the same posture of praying, eyes lifted up, knees bowed down, as though I prayed to God; and if God or his angels should ask me when I thought last of God in that prayer, I cannot tell. Sometimes I find that I had forgot what I was about, but when I began to forget it I cannot tell. A memory of yesterday's pleasures, a fear of tomorrow's dangers, a straw under my knee, a noise in mine ear, a light in mine eye, an anything, a nothing, a fancy, a chimera in my brain troubles me in my prayer[70]

The religious subject, and the seriousness with which Donne handles his sense of inadequacy in worshipping God, do not stop him from arranging his ideas and his phrases in eloquent ways. Andrewes' style is more measured, but equally deliberate in its deployment of rhetorical craft and striking imagery:

> Christ rising was indeed a gardener, and that a strange one, Who made such an herb grow out of the ground this day as the like was never seen before, a dead body to shoot forth alive out of the grave. I ask, was He so this day alone? No, but this profession of His, this day begun, He will follow to the end. For He it is That by virtue of this morning's act shall garden our bodies too, turn all our graves into garden plots; yea, shall one day turn land and sea and all into a great garden, and so husband them as they shall in due time bring forth live bodies, even all our bodies alive again.[71]

In fact, at around the time Buchan and Kipling were speculating on the literary qualities of the King James Bible, the poet T.S. Eliot was writing about Lancelot Andrewes and proposing him as a great lost talent in English literary history. Eliot suggested he was less suited to a general readership than Donne, and "will never have many readers in any one generation", but was nonetheless a superb prose writer with a distinctive style:

> It is only when we have saturated ourselves in his prose, followed the movement of his thought, that we find his examination of words terminating in the ecstasy of assent. Andrews takes a word and derives the world from it; squeezing and squeezing the word until it yields a full juice of meaning which we should never have supposed any word to possess.[72]

Eliot quotes another critic approvingly, who praises Andrewes' "constructive force", "fire" and "poetic structure", and himself refers to the preacher's "extraordinary prose" and "flashes phrases which never desert the memory". Thus Buchan and Kipling's wondering about the absence of "writers" from the origins of the King James Bible, despite its enormous literary value, took place at around the time when Eliot was encouraging literary readers to appreciate the qualities of Andrewes as a prose stylist. The world of fiction and journalism which Kipling and Buchan inhabited was very different from the church of Shakespeare's time, but there were plenty of people involved in the latter who had a daily and professional concern with the power of words.

To shed more light on *Proofs of Holy Writ*, and the sort of fiction that is taking place here, I think we can draw connections with one of Kipling's more famous works: *Puck of Pook's Hill*, mentioned above in the quotation about Kipling's "Demon". This series of fantasy short stories was published in 1906, and it relates the encounter of a group of contemporary children with a goblin-like creature called Puck. The Shakespearean associations of the title are developed more strongly in the first story, in which the children perform a shortened version of *A Midsummer Night's Dream* on Midsummer Eve. Pleased with their success in remembering all the lines, they run through the play twice more, with the following result:

> The bushes parted. In the very spot where Dan had stood as Puck they saw a small, brown, pointy-eared person with a snub nose, slanting blue eyes and a grin that ran right across his freckled face. He shaded his forehead as though he were watching Quince, Snout, Bottom and the others rehearsing *Pyramus and Thisbe*, and, in a voice as Three Cows asking to be milked, he began:
>
> "What hempen homespuns have we swaggering here, So near the cradle of our fairy Queen?"
>
> He stopped, hollowed one hand around his ear, and, with a wicked twinkle in his eye, went on:
>
> "What, a play towards? I'll be an auditor;
> An actor too, perhaps, if I see cause."
>
> The children looked and gasped. The small thing—he was no taller than Dan's shoulder—stepped quietly into the Ring.
>
> "I'm rather out of practice," he said; "but that's the way my part ought to be played."[73]

It becomes clear that the children have accidentally summoned up Puck himself, by performing their *Midsummer Night's Dream* three times on Midsummer Eve at a place called "Pook's Hill". "By Oak, Ash and Thorn!", the creature tells them, "If this had happened a few hundred years ago you'd have had all the People of the Hills out like bees in June!" Puck arranges for the children to meet people from English history, such as a Norman knight and a Roman centurion, who tell their own stories of what happened in the landscape around Pook's Hill over thousands of years.

In *Puck of Pook's Hill* Shakespeare literally provides words to conjure with (even if the children didn't intentionally use them for that purpose). Immersing themselves in Shakespeare's language, and in the English countryside, the children find their way into both the world of magic and the world of history. As they perform *A Midsummer Night's Dream*, they create a link between their own reality and the realms which Puck inhabits. It is striking that Puck enters speaking the lines which Shakespeare assigns him in the play and refers to "my part", as if he is both himself and playing the role which Shakespeare created (a role which involves interrupting amateur theatricals by the Athenian workmen in the original play). The book suggests, at least in a fantastical way, that Shakespeare's words have the power to connect the past and present, and even the mundane and the supernatural world. This is not simply a matter of Shakespeare's texts being very old, since many of the stories in the book are set in eras before Shakespeare's own lifetime. There is a sense in *Puck of Pook's Hill* that Shakespeare allows the children to connect with the deep realities of the English landscape and its history. They discover that "Pook's Hill" is a name derived from Puck, and that the world around them is part of a much larger story being played out over centuries. This is all meant non-literally, of course. The story is explicitly fantastical, and it involves a playful approach to the past. Puck tells the children, for example, that the Old Gods have fled Britain partly because many of them had been brought by people like the Vikings or the Phoenicians, and they couldn't get used to the weather. The sterner and more bloodthirsty gods did themselves a disservice, he explains, because demanding sacrifices of animals or humans means that eventually the worshippers will get fed up and let the temple fall apart from neglect. Some gods took to being more minor supernatural creatures such as water-spirits, or hanging around in trees and moaning at passers-by as eerie presences, or simply left the land.

All this is humorous historical fantasy of the kind likely to be familiar to many readers from Terry Pratchett's novels over recent decades. But it is also an account of the development of religious beliefs and folklore which parallels a lot of scholarly and popular discussion around the turn of the century.[74] Many people in Edwardian England did think that folk customs like maypole dancing and folk stories about creatures like boggarts and kelpies could be analysed for the remnants of ancient religious beliefs which they contained. The "Green Man", for example, whose face appeared surrounded by leaves in church decorations and pub signs, was identified by many as a pre-Christian nature god. Ronald Hutton has discussed these beliefs in the context of a "tremendous idealization of rural England which ... reached an apogee between 1880 and 1930;

indeed it might be called a plateau, as it has not diminished significantly since", and connects them to a major demographic shift: "a single and simple process; that in 1810 about 80 per cent of English people lived in the countryside, and by 1910 about 80 per cent lived in towns". In this situation, writers such as Thomas Hardy, Kenneth Grahame and Kipling himself became fascinated by the countryside as a mysterious source of ancient traditions, oral culture and half-obscured survivals from pagan times (an attitude which tended to increase when most writers and readers were no longer actually living in the countryside, nor regularly meeting the country people whom they regarded as the unconscious carriers of these ancient traditions). Figures like the Green Man seemed to offer the possibility of cultural archaeology, as urban intellectuals sought to dig through the appearances on pub signs and church doors, down into the deep symbolism of the figure and its supposed roots in pagan and Celtic culture. Kipling's story playfully literalised these ideas, as if the Green Man had given up being a nature spirit and taken to easier work standing on church pillars or helping out at the local pub. This points to a sophisticated engagement with the ideas of history, myth and narrative, in which the author presents the audience with fictional elements which cannot literally be true, alongside historical anecdotes which are clearly based in recorded history (even if those stories themselves did not actually take place), as well as a light-hearted engagement with previous attempts to dig through the British past in search of supernatural creatures.

Puck of Pook's Hill shows more explicitly a mode of fiction which I believe we can also see operating in "Proofs of Holy Writ": a use of history and myth woven together around the English countryside. Both works show Kipling scripting impossible conversations and staging supernatural events to approach a more profound level of truth. "Proofs of Holy Writ" is a deliberately playful text which doesn't purport to tell a factual or accurate version of history, but uses traces from the past to weave a fantastical meditation upon history and its relationship to us. Though I have stressed the professional and practical element of the story above, setting it in the context of Kipling and Buchan's working lives as writers, there is also a pastoral strain to the tale. It begins with the line "They seated themselves in the heavy chairs on the pebbled floor beneath the eaves of the summer-house by the orchard", and the passage I quoted above recounts Will walking "towards a tree in the orchard, turning again, when he had reached it, by a well-worn track through the grass", where he demands privacy as he paces and speaks aloud and waits for his "Demon".

There is a sense of an enchanted landscape here, just as in Puck of Pook's Hill, with a character gesturing and chanting Shakespeare's words to summon up a supernatural force from around them. (Of course in this version the person chanting Shakespeare's words is Shakespeare, and he fully intends for the Demon to come, unlike the accidental summoning of Puck by the children.) It is not amongst the theatres of the Bankside in London, or the royal Court, that Shakespeare and Jonson complete their task in "Proofs of Holy Writ", but in an English orchard (with all the Biblical implications of knowledge, excitement and danger implied by the apples lying near).

Enchanted English landscapes were part of Kipling's personal literary vision, and a major context of English writing at the time. As Hutton comments, Kipling spent his formative years in India and much of his adult life outside England, so for him "the eternal and essential England represented a ... distant fantasy". Kipling's playful meditations upon the magic and mystery of English history and the English landscape were partly a result of his outsider's view of it, and "when he eventually retired to Sussex, he described it as 'the most wonderful foreign land I have ever been in.'"[75]

Thus "Proofs of Holy Writ" offers an illuminatingly different kind of myth about Shakespeare and the King James Bible to the Psalm 46 legend, weaving a deliberately fantastical narrative from images of English history and the English landscape. Though there is little supernatural about it, the story almost has the air of fantasy fiction, as Kipling indulges in a conscious flight of fantasy, imagining a moment when the connection which should have existed between Shakespeare and the King James Bible actually took place. The next chapter will explore the appearance of the Psalm 46 legend in a non-fictional context—a Biblical commentary—but which also frames the story on the edge of myth.

The Story is Told...

Despite the scholarly disputes discussed in earlier chapters, the Psalm 46 legend continues to appear in print. The most recent example I have found appears in the *New International Commentary on the Old Testament* produced by the major US publisher Eerdmans in 2014. The entry for Psalm 46 contains an account of various technical and religious questions to help the reader understand and appreciate it better: for example, the origins and meaning of epithet "the LORD of hosts" is discussed, and the water imagery is related to other Old Testament water imagery and to the Babylonian religious text the *Enuma Elish*. The commentary concludes with a devotional reflection, declaring that "in the midst of our tumultuous, chaotic modern world, Psalm 46 reminds us that God can calm the raging seas and the trembling mountains, and turn them to rivers of life and calm dwelling places" and advises the reader that "all is required of us is that we *stand still* and acknowledge the God who is *with* us". Amidst this expected combination of analysis and devotion, the commentary includes this passage, which I will quote in full:

A wonderful legendary story exists about Psalm 46. According to the tale, the translators of the King James Version, who worked in 1604–11 C.E., were determined to arrive at the best possible English translation of the biblical text. When they considered the translation of the poetic material of the Old Testament, especially the book of Psalms, they felt the best choice for a translator was none other than England's own poet and playwright of the time, William Shakespeare. And so they prevailed upon him to work with them in rendering the psalms into good English. Shakespeare agreed and undertook the task. One by one the psalms were transformed from their enigmatic Hebrew and Latin predecessors to the lively English of Shakespeare's day. Serendipitously, Shakespeare arrived at the translation of Psalm 46 on the day of his 46th birthday. Not one to let a good opportunity pass by, Shakespeare decided to 'leave his mark' on the Psalter to mark the occasion. The words cooperated, and when readers examine the King James translation of Psalm 46, they discover an interesting phenomenon. The 46th word from the beginning of the text of Psalm 46 is 'shake': ('though the mountains shake,' v.3); the 46th word from the end of the text of Psalm 46 is 'spear': ('he cutteth the spear in sunder,' v.9) – an enduring tribute to the 46th birthday of England's great poet laureate. Thus, according to the legend, Shakespeare, the master poet of the sixteenth and seventeenth centuries, lent his immeasurable talent to the English Bible translation that was the standard for the English Protestant church for over three hundred years.[76]

In light of the investigations in earlier chapters, there are obvious problems with this account: the idea that translators would have thought it appropriate to employ a playwright to translate the Psalms, the assumption that the wording in the King James Bible is the result of the Psalms going directly from Hebrew and Latin to English, and the suggestion that the "best" version of them would be one written by a poet. More interesting, however, is the question of why this story is still being told in a commentary on the Psalms. What impression does this give, and what function does it fulfil? Put more directly, how does this story work and what point is it trying to prove?

In analysing how this version of the legend works, the first point to notice is contained in the first four words: "a wonderful legendary story". The commentary does not specifically claim that this is true, it identifies it as "legendary" and a "story", assigning it a lesser authority than the discussion of Hebrew names or literary parallels. On the other hand, it repeats the story in detail, rather than mentioning it as a myth or an inaccurate fable which some people incorrectly believe about this psalm. At the most basic level, the commentary must regard the legend as valuable in some sense, since it takes the trouble to repeat it, and to draw out the conclusion that "according to the legend" the King James Bible was edified by "the immeasurable talent" of Shakespeare and went on to be "the standard for the English Protestant church for over three hundred years".

The story is told …

This presentation of the story as worth pondering, without asserting its specific historical accuracy, is reminiscent of another use of narrative in Christian writing and speaking: the sermon anecdote. Many people who listen to sermons in British and American churches, or read Christian devotional books, will be familiar with the introduction of a short anecdote to illustrate a point. This often takes the form of short narrative which involves unnamed characters in an unspecified location, relying more on the moral qualities of the story, and its potential to inspire the congregation (or reader), than the historical specifics.

There is a formula which frequently appears to introduce this kind of narrative, particularly in the Evangelical Protestant tradition: "the story is told…".

A few examples of this phrase give a sense of the ways the formula is used, and the kinds of narratives it can introduce:

> The story is told about how a man took his new hunting dog on a trial hunt one day. After a while he managed to shoot a duck and it fell in the lake. The dog walked over the water, picked up the duck, and brought it to his master.[77]

> The story is told of one minister who was invited to preach a trial sermon in a vacant pulpit, but who refused, saying that the pulpit committee must hear him in his own church. "I am like these matches," the minister said, "that won't strike fire except on the box they come in."[78]

> The story is told of a church member who was asked to read the nativity story of Luke 2 at the Christmas morning service. As she stood to read, she began by saying, "Now stop me if you've heard this before…"[79]

As you can see from these examples, the "story" in question tends to be rather blurry about the specifics of location, date and characters. It can be striking or mundane, but always has a moral point to make, which the preacher can draw out for their listeners. It is tempting to suggest (though I have only an anecdotal basis for this speculation) that the stories introduced by "the story is told..." in the Evangelical Protestant tradition serve similar purposes to the lives of the saints in the Catholic tradition, or the haggadic narratives about the rabbis in the Jewish tradition. They provide a space for narratives which reflect on the principles and ideas found in the Scriptures, and connect theological and moral ideas to people's lives. "The story is told..." might supply a similar function to begin "When St. Anthony was visited by one of the monks in the desert...", or "When Caesar heard that the food on the shabbat had a special taste...", in bringing the resources of narrative to bear on the point being considered, whilst locating them within a religious framework.

"The story is told" provides a way of presenting a story which does not absolutely assert the historical accuracy of the anecdote, but allows the congregation to hear it and reflect on the moral message it contains. It gives the preacher a chance to relate a narrative in a mode which is possibly fictional but possibly true, and still contains value, without impinging on the absolute truth accorded to the Bible, which is also likely to be quoted and discussed in the same sermon.[80]

The commentary's introduction of the Psalm 46 legend by calling it "a wonderful legendary story" seems to carry out the same function. It lays out the narrative without asserting its historical accuracy, which—as we have seen—is a good thing, since Shakespeare was never the poet laureate, there is no evidence that the translators knew him, the words previously existed in those positions, etc. Nonetheless, by asserting that the story "exists" and telling it, it allows the reader to enjoy the legend and take from it the message which the commentary intends. As I suggested above, these stories always seem to have a fairly definite meaning adduced by the preacher at the end, and this one follows the same pattern. If the sermon anecdote is how this example of the legend seems to work, further attention to the commentary can reveal what it is trying to achieve.

The Shakespeare Bible

The meaning of this particular version of the legend is signalled by the way the story is set up, and the conclusion drawn from it at the end: it offers both a motive for the translators' actions and a point to the story. The motive in question was their determination "to arrive at the best possible English translation of the biblical text", and a conviction that "the best choice for a translator was none other than England's own poet and playwright of the time", leading them to ask Shakespeare "to work with them in rendering the psalms into good English". At the other end of the narrative, it concludes that "the master poet" Shakespeare "lent his immeasurable talent" to the King James Bible, which "was the standard for the English Protestant church for over three hundred years". There is a particular stress laid here on the quality of the King James Bible, but on its literary qualities rather than its linguistic accuracy or theological trustworthiness. Shakespeare's help in putting the psalms into "good English" shows a concern with the style of the translation, which the emphasis on his poetic abilities and vast talent extends. Both the motive for

Shakespeare's involvement, and the conclusion drawn from the outcome, are focused on how literary and stylish the resulting English psalms are.

I have discussed in a previous chapter why I do not think this is a particularly convincing part of the legend as a whole—both because the King James Bible drew heavily on previous versions, and because it compares unfavourably with more consciously poetic English translations of the Psalms at the time—but it is striking to find it as the focus of the story in a commentary on the Old Testament. This story offers us a specifically Shakespearean Bible, and it is worth considering why.

The key to this version of the legend lies in the changing attitudes towards both Shakespeare and the Bible during the centuries which intervene between the translation of the King James Bible and the appearance of the Eerdmans' commentary. From the late 17th century onwards, Shakespeare's reputation grew: at various points he was a popular playwright from an earlier era, a collection of plays useful for making political points, an image of British national identity, the epitome of artistic excellence, and even a divinely inspired creator whose works encapsulated the very nature of humanity and existence.[81] By the late 19th century, Shakespeare was held in extraordinarily high esteem, with George Bernard Shaw irritably coining the term "Bardolatry" for what seemed to him the almost cultish veneration of the poet and his works amongst British people.

Alongside this remarkable rise in the respect accorded to the works of Shakespeare, the later 19th century saw something of a crisis in attitudes towards the Bible. The most famous aspect of this was the advances in science—first in geology, then in biology—which presented an alternative view of the Creation story to that which the Bible seemed to present.

For a Victorian Christian the Genesis narratives might give a sense that God had specifically and deliberately created every part of the world they saw around them, that when they enjoyed the beauty of nature they were contemplating the handiwork of God in some sense, and that the order of the natural world placed humans at the top of an immutable and divinely-ordained hierarchy. These understandings of the world could be seriously shaken by scientific discoveries which might suggest instead that nature was violent, rapacious, competitive and amoral, that humans' place in the world was accidental (and subject to change), and that God exercised sovereignty through a brutal administrative system instead of a personal loving care.

Even on the level of Biblical language, the imagery of hills and mountains (themselves found in Psalm 46) could not quite ever mean the same thing to a culture who had discovered that those mountains had not been standing firm since the beginning of time, but were themselves in a state of definite—if incredibly slow—flux and degeneration.[82] The disorienting and unsettling effect of these discoveries is demonstrated by the question which was allegedly asked by Bishop Wilberforce of the scientist Thomas Huxley during a debate at the Oxford University Museum in 1860, as to whether Huxley, since he believed in Darwin's theories, claimed to be descended from a monkey on his grandmother's side or his grandfather's side.

There is some doubt amongst historians as to whether this question was actually posed in the discussion, or whether it was phrased in a rather more Victorian way, but the fact that people believed Wilberforce had asked Huxley this question shows the potentially enormous impact which evolution could have on people's sense of who they were and what their lives meant. This was less a controversy over the abstract facts of scientific history thousands of years ago, and more an argument about the meaning of each individual human. After all, Wilberforce's alleged question is personal to the point of serious insult: it is the Victorian equivalent of the bishop retorting to the eminent scientist "Yeah, but I heard your mum is…" Though it wasn't simply the "accuracy" of the Bible which science challenged, this was often the way the issue was framed. Through the early 20th century (with events such as the Scopes Monkey Trials) and to this day, those who reject scientific theories because they contradict particular forms of Christian teaching tend to explain their opposition as based on "what the Bible says".

The Bible was also undergoing a serious reassessment in light of the Biblical scholarship which expanded and became more generally accessible during the later 19th century. These critical projects included the identification of four different "sources" within the early books of the Old Testament, and the scrutiny of the differing ways in which the Gospels told the story of the life and death of Jesus. Both investigations suggested that the text as we possess it was the result of a complex process of editing, rewriting, combining sources, ongoing theological reflection and church politics. One of the great religious projects of this era was the "Quest for the Historical Jesus", in which scholars attempted to get behind the Gospels' theological emphases and make out the historical events and speeches which lay behind the later religious development.

Though these projects were often undertaken by Christians with a devout concern for religious truth, they were seen by many others as impious, destructive and casting doubt on the "truth" of the Bible. As with the scientific discoveries, it may well be that people's disquiet was less focused around the literal truth of particular details (such as how many blind men Jesus healed, or how old Hagar's son was), and more about the general trustworthiness of the Biblical text. Suggesting that there were a number of documents lying behind the Old and New Testaments, whose outlines could be dimly perceived through inconsistencies, shifts in style, and varying theologies, involved suggesting that the Bible was not entirely unique, perfect and unlike any other book. Saying that the Bible was the result of a process of development and editing also raised the possibility that the Bible might continue to change, and was not finished and completed for all time. (There is an obvious parallel here with the way the ideas of geology and evolution threatened assumptions about change and permanence in the world.)

It is not necessary to point to particular doctrines or beliefs which would need to change in the wake of such Biblical scholarship in order to appreciate how unsettling it might have been to Christians used to a more traditional attitude towards the Bible. When the Oxford theologian Benjamin Jowett wrote that the

Bible should be read "like any other book", he meant that it should be read with as few preconceptions as possible, in order to appreciate the true meaning of the words, and not the religious assumptions or later beliefs which might intervene between the reader and the text. However, treating the Bible "like any other book" could easily sound like questioning the entire basis of the Christian faith for many people. After this double crisis in traditional attitudes to the Bible, the 20th century saw a drop in the book's relative importance in the public sphere. As religious pluralism became more widespread in Anglo-American culture, and public institutions became less consciously part of a Christian tradition, the Bible became less the symbol of social cohesion and moral values, and more the central text of a number of religious groups. It is a somewhat sweeping statement to declare that the Bible simply became less important over the 20th century, but it is certainly true that it was not accorded the kind of official and public status at the end of this period than it had been during the years of Queen Victoria.

One specific set of examples could be found in the court cases in the US during the late 20th and early 21st century, in which public institutions were challenged for displaying the Ten Commandments. In *Stone vs Graham* in 1980, the US Supreme Court ruled that Kentucky could not require every state-funded school classroom to put a copy of the Commandments on the wall, whilst the first decade of the 21st century saw a series of cases across Texas, Alabama, Tennessee and Oklahoma (amongst other states) which centred on court houses or City Halls setting up monuments with the Commandments engraved upon them. Aside from the legalities of the separation of church and state and the questions of constitutional law involved, it is clear that displaying a Biblical text in a public place was perceived as making powerful assertions about religion and its connection to the surrounding society. The Bible—in this case a set of statements derived from the law-codes of the Old Testament—was a powerful symbol for what some people saw as vital American values and which others opposed as inimical to freedom and liberal democracy.

This century of change in attitudes to the Bible resulted in a variety of different responses from those who still read the Bible and considered it significant. One was represented by the growing strength of conservative and even fundamentalist forms of Christianity, especially in America, which often took pride in asserting their opposition to "modern" and "secular" society and in contrasting these with their adherence to "Biblical" values. Another reaction could be seen in the development of liberal theologies, with their emphasis on the Bible as a record of human religious experience, and as a collection of powerful symbols which could help people make sense of the world (even if they were not literally historically true.) Yet another attitude appeared in the tendency to discuss the Bible in literary terms, as a treasury of artistic achievement and human inspiration, which held value aside from its claims to theological truth or religious usefulness. Regarding the Bible as literature was a controversial attitude in some quarters.

As I noted above, applying the same categories to the Bible as to other books could be seen as questioning its unique status and its claims to truth. However, it could also be seen—even by relatively conservative groups—as putting the Bible in its rightful place within the cultural and educational spheres. Looking at how the Bible was made up of literary forms, and tracing its influence on later artworks might seem trivial to some, but to others it demonstrated the deep connection between Christianity and the English-speaking culture of the last ten centuries. The "Great Books" courses offered by some US universities and colleges from the 1920s onwards encouraged this sort of thinking, deliberately marshalling together the key works which an educated person might be supposed to need, and the Bible found a robust place amongst them.

It appears on the "National Great Books Curriculum" which received funding from the National Endowment for the Arts, and in the syllabi of "Great Books" courses from Thomas Aquinas College in California, to Gutenberg College in Oregon. The Great Books programme at Mercer University, which includes the Bible alongside works by Plato, Shakespeare, Marx, Austen, Descartes and others, is predicated on the idea that:

> The Western tradition is both the ground and the source of the conditions necessary for the very possibility and continuation of our republic. Each generation of citizens must engage and confront for itself the tradition that it claims to inherit. A tradition (as the Latin trāditio suggests) can either be "handed down" as a gift or "handed over" as a betrayal. True inheritance of such a tradition comes through understanding, which is only made possible by serious study.

Thus the Bible could be valued in an educational context which did not explicitly advance its religious claims or its spiritual value, on the grounds of its moral and philosophical quality, but also its foundational status for contemporary Western/US culture. This relatively conservative approach finds a counterpart in the more liberal or progressive universities and colleges, too, via the blend of high and low culture characteristic of postmodernism. The continuing presence of Biblical tropes, characters, narratives and influences in popular culture provides a fertile ground for the kind of research which values the popular and the everyday.

Despite this shift in value, pointing out influence is a way of asserting the power of the original text, and the same is true when it comes to popular culture. Finding

Biblical echoes everywhere from medieval ballads to *Buffy the Vampire Slayer* emphasises the importance of the Bible in understanding the cultural world available to contemporary consumers, even on a pragmatic level.

As Yvonne Sherwood and Stephen D. Moore put it:

> The mantra of the Bible as the book that Western culture cannot get over or around finds its consummate expression in biblical cultural studies, whether through analysis of the biblical in the paintings of Rembrandt, William Blake or Samuel Bak; operatic libretto, Bach's cantatas, or the lyrics of US; *The Passion of the Christ* or *The Life of Brian*; or the political rhetoric of Margret Thatcher or George W. Bush.[83]

This stress on the value of reading the Bible as literature was accompanied in some quarters by an emphasis on its literary value. Northrop Frye's study *The Great Code: The Bible and Literature* asserted in the 1980s that "a student of English literature who does not know the Bible does not understand a good deal of what is going on in what he read", that "[t]he Bible is clearly a major element in our own imaginative traditions, whatever we may think we believed about it" and that "[m]any issues in critical theory today had their origin in the hermeneutic study of the Bible".[84]

This reads unequivocally as a claim for authority: the Bible is not only a significant subject for literary study, but a subject which controls the correct understanding of other literature. From this position a move is possible into extolling the Bible *as* literature, in implicit or explicit comparison with other literary writings. Literature was not only a category into which the Bible could be put, but a category which could demonstrate its greatness. The shift between "it is valuable to read the Bible in a literary way" to "the Bible has literary value" is easily made, and the two statements overlap to a certain extent. It does not take much development to move on to "literature is a way of showing that the Bible is more valuable than other books" or "literary readings prove the Bible to be right". In this way the literary approach to the Bible is attractive to two groups which often disagree otherwise: liberal readers who may see literary value as more significant than theological or historical accuracy, and conservative readers who may see the Bible's literary qualities as evidence that it is supreme in all areas of human life.

Various modern books on the Bible intended for a popular audience display this tendency to use "literature" as a category to elevate the Bible. For example, a recent book on the Psalms by the influential scholar and clergyman N.T. Wright invites the reader to indulge in a thought experiment:

> Suppose the Psalms had been lost and had never been printed in any Bibles or prayer books. Suppose they turned up in a faded but still legible scroll, discovered by archaeologists in the sands of Jordan or Egypt. What would happen? When deciphered and translated, they would be on the front page of every newspaper in the world. Many scholars from many disciplines would marvel at the beauty and content of these ancient worship songs and poems.[85]

Some readers might want to quibble at the details of this imaginary scenario, especially if they work in archaeology or literary studies. The translation of ancient poetry, however excellent, rarely finds its way onto the front pages of newspapers, and university scholars don't spend much of their professional life using a text's "beauty" as a central critical category. That aside, it is striking that Wright imagines the Psalms' beauty making them famous and putting them on the agenda of the world media. Though they are often read through the lens of Christian belief, the Psalms do not contain the central message of Christianity: they do not proclaim the "good news" of salvation in the overt way that the Gospels or the Epistles of Paul do. There is no suggestion here that the Psalms would be famous because they proclaim the rescue of humanity from sin, or announce the birth of the Son of God, or any of the other messages which might be identified as crucial to the meaning of Christianity. It is their quality as inspiring literature which seems to constitute their claim on the attention of the world in Wright's imagined example.

A less famous author demonstrates a similar set of assumption in a more obvious way in *The Bible As Literary Treasure*, which declares that the Psalms "are among the oldest poems in the world, and they still rank with any poetry in any culture, ancient or modern, from anywhere in the world". The poetic qualities of the Psalms are not offered here as a way of understanding their meaning better, nor as a historical fact which can develop our sense of how they might have been written or performed, but as a standard by which their value can be judged. This is immediately translated into a way to "rank" the poems, and to assert that the Bible contains poetry which is as good as any which can be found elsewhere. The same impulse can be seen in the declaration that Deborah's song in the Book of Judges "has been described by a modern critic as; 'a song of force and fire that is worthy to be placed alongside the noblest battle odes in any language'". Literature is invoked as a way to assure the reader that the Bible is as good and as important as any non-Biblical writing, and a "modern critic" is cited as evidence that experts in this area endorse the judgement. The point of this literary discussion becomes plain with the author's statement that:

> We need to recover the truth that the Bible is a lively, dynamic book that is just as interesting to read as the latest travel narrative or a well-written novel. The Bible contains essays, epigrams, treatises, histories, sermons, legal documents, dramas, love songs, national anthems, war ballads, letters, orations, hymns of defeat and triumph, pilgrim songs, chants, riddles, fanciful acrostics, and indeed every other form of literary expression.[86]

The issue of the Bible's status as literature—and the connected question of its literary value—is used here to make an argument for why people should read the Bible more. The Bible is placed alongside other works of literature not in order to call its unique qualities into question or to suggest that other books could provide the same value to the reader, but to argue that the Bible is at the top of any possible scale of value. Anything books can do, the Bible can do better, or at least as well. Framing the Bible as a literary work becomes a way of aggrandising it, and suggesting that people do not hold it in high enough esteem.

This is the attitude which I think can be discerned in the Eerdmans' *Commentary on the Old Testament*, though in a much less dramatic way. The version of the Psalm 46 legend told here stresses the "good English" of the King James Bible, and notes that it apparently contains the work of a "master poet" with an extraordinary talent. By connecting the King James Bible with Shakespeare, it associates the Psalms with poetry which is far more revered and influential in most English-speaking culture. I would suggest that the Bible actually gains authority and prestige from this association, linking the Christian Scriptures with an author who is often held up as the absolute paragon of literary value.

Though the commentary does not specifically vouch for the historical truth of the legend, it reprints it in a way which encourages the reader to imagine Shakespeare and the Psalms as equivalently "literary". The phrase "good English" has multiple implications in this context, even though they may not have been specifically intended by the writers of the commentary. It distinguishes the King James Bible from the Latin versions of the Bible which had been in use before the Reformation, marking it as a distinctively Protestant undertaking which fits with the Evangelical emphasis on making the Bible and its message available to everyone. Secondly, it connects reading the Bible to social standing: speaking "good English" is associated in much of US society with education, public culture and social aspiration. Thirdly, it claims the same status for the Bible as the literary classics which act as a touchstone of value in US schools and colleges, and in the more informal literary cultures of journalism and reviewing. If the King James Bible is "good English" and contains valuable literature, it should be grouped with *The Great Gatsby*, *To Kill A Mockingbird*, Shakespeare's plays and the other works of recognised literary quality.

On examination, the appearance of the Psalm 46 legend in the *New International Commentary on the Old Testament* seems to stem from two tendencies in Anglo-American Christianity over the last century or so. The first is the use of devotional anecdotes in preaching and writing, which don't necessarily have any factual or historical basis, but which are seen as useful because of the moral message they convey. The Eerdmans' commentary introduces the legend with a curiously ambiguous formula that "a wonderful legendary story exists", neither claiming the truth of the tale nor dismissing it, but giving it space in the book because of the value it has for devout readers of the Bible. The second tendency is the move towards reading the Bible as literature, and of using literary quality to assert the value and importance of the Biblical texts. The commentary associates the Psalms with an author whose global supremacy is unequalled by any other writer in English, an enormously powerful name in world culture.

In doing so, it implies that—as others have explicitly stated—the Bible is remarkable for its "secular" literary qualities as well as its sacred character, and that it should be read for enjoyment as well as duty.

Though it tells a story about the activities of 17th-century writers and churchmen, which was probably invented in the late 19th century, this version of the legend is clearly reusing the story for the specific demands of Evangelical Protestant readers in the early 21st century. The legend has a distinct meaning in this context, just as it has a different meaning in the 1890s and the 1930s. The legend's basic outline may remain the same, but its implications depend upon how it is told, by whom, and what they hope to achieve by telling it.

Having traced its arc through the 20th century, I will consider in the next chapter what its overall implications might be, what view of the world the legend might reflect, and why people continue to tell it.

The Lure of the Legend

The previous chapters have laid out a response to the Psalm 46 legend in two different directions. I have discussed the historical, textual and literary reasons why I think the legend is not only unproved but deeply unlikely. I hope my arguments have been reasonable, and based on the evidence available to us about the context of both Shakespeare's works and the translation of the King James Bible. I must admit that I have felt it difficult at times to argue against the legend along the accepted lines of scholarly debate, since the legend itself seems not to be proceeding along those lines (or perhaps "playing by those rules" would be a better phrase).

In marshalling the evidence against the idea that Shakespeare helped write the Authorized Version I sometimes felt at a slight disadvantage compared to my usual scholarly work, since I cannot see that there is any evidence that he did, and so it is difficult to address that evidence. Nonetheless, I have treated it as a possible hypothesis, and tried to set it within the historical literature about the early 17th century, in order to show how far it does not fit. As I mentioned in the prologue,

I do not suggest that the legend is totally impossible. It purports to be a theory about a group of people who were alive in the same country at the same time, and a collection of texts which were familiar to all of them.

The Psalms of the King James Bible are a set of Early Modern poems (in some sense), and Shakespeare was an Early Modern poet. His involvement in the project does not require any suspension of the laws of historical causation as we understand them: we do not have to posit that Shakespeare somehow influenced the temple psalms of Israel despite living centuries and centuries after their composition and compilation. Nor do we need to involve any of forms of intervention which mainstream historiography has ruled out: aliens do not need to have borrowed the manuscripts of the psalms, nor does Shakespeare need to have seen the poems in a vision. From this point of view, the theory is positively plausible, and if documents turned up proving it to be accurate I would be both intrigued and delighted, though this book would need a bit of rewriting.

Indeed, if a better and more erudite scholar than me (and there are at least 12 of those within a casual stone's throw of the desk at which I am writing this sentence) showed that in fact the evidence we possess does support the theory, I would be willing to listen and be persuaded if I could see their point. It is simply that, at the moment, it seems so extremely unlikely that I can rule it out of my mental picture of England in the early 17th century.

If it were true, I would not only have to accept it as a fact, but I would also need to reassess the aspects of history which rule it out as a reasonable possibility. If the theory were accurate, it would not simply add another fact to the accumulation of data we possess about the early 17th century, but would have an impact on our interpretation of other data: we would have to ask whether we had been right in our understanding of social attitudes towards the theatre, of the history of the Biblical text in English, of poetic practice in the period, and various of the topics I have discussed in previous chapters. All of this is possible, but it would involve bringing the Psalm 46 legend within the ambit of historical and literary scholarship, and asking how it affected that mesh of narratives and debates.

Given that there is no serious evidence for the legend, beyond the numerical coincidence (which needs some selective misreading to make it persuasive), why is the Psalm 46 legend attractive? Why are people willing to believe it, and why does it continue to crop up in different forms? The specific examples I have examined in the previous chapters suggest some particular reasons and some general trends. The story seemed plausible in the late 19th century because Shakespeare's reputation as both a writer and a transcendent genius coincided which the enormous respect accorded to the King James Bible as more than simply a good translation of the Bible. Their parallel arcs through history collided in a story that suggested they had been connected all along. The Kipling story showed a gifted author musing on the great literary reputations of the two texts, and using them to reflect on his own personal form of literary inspiration and his feelings about the history of the English landscape. Kipling's short story imaginatively reconstructed the Early Modern period via his own experience of mysterious textual creation, and (conveniently) placed his works in the line of inspired writings which included Shakespeare's plays and the King James Bible. The entry in the Bible commentary demonstrated Shakespeare being used to emphasise the literary qualities of the Bible, and to assert the religious text's connection with a touchstone of cultural value. After a 20th century in which the Bible had become less central to the public cultures of Britain and the US, this retelling of the story placed the Bible in the context of education, literary value and social aspiration.

Beyond these individual cases I think there are suggestions we can make about the appeal of this legend. This is not to suggest that everyone who found the story compelling or believed it did so for the reasons I am proposing, nor that doing so involves signing up to a complete set of cultural and political beliefs. Nonetheless, I think the Psalm 46 legend sits within a particular set of narratives about the past and cultural values, both expressing them and reinforcing them in a minor way. It connects two literary and religious artefacts from the past, providing a narrative which explains how they were related.

On this level it undertakes the same work as the historical scholarship which I've suggested disproves the legend, in a different way. Given that these two collections of texts have survived from the same period, some explanation of their relationship is reasonable, and the Psalm 46 story gives one kind of explanation. It does so, moreover, in a way which fits conveniently with a modern view of the texts, which adds to its appeal as a narrative. It does not require the listener to adjust their sense that the King James Bible and the works of Shakespeare are the most important books from this period, nor to imagine a past in which this was not obviously the case. This is part of the problem with the legend from a historical point of view, but I suspect it is also part of its appeal in the present. It offers a story which projects the modern situation of these texts as cultural landmarks into the past, and implies that our attitudes and ideas are sanctioned by the testimony of that past. Relatedly, it implies that the canon of texts which exists currently—the group of books which are studied, taught, read and regarded as possessing surpassing cultural and literary value—is both correct and sufficient. Correct because this group of books (or Shakespeare and the Bible, their pre-eminent members and representatives) is apparently not subject to the vagaries of time or fashion: they were the most important texts 400 years ago, and they remain so now. Sufficient because the story builds a connection between the texts which both binds them more tightly together, and which does not require any other text or context in order to make sense. We do not need to delve into the lives of Laurence Chaderton, (of whom we have never heard) or scrutinise the Sternhold and Hopkins Psalter (which is arguably not very good) in order for the Psalm 46 legend to work. The texts with which we are already familiar are the most significant ones, and all the necessary texts have survived. If Shakespeare (in some small way) explains the Bible, and vice versa, then the canon is in that same way reinforced in both its internal connections and its external boundaries. The Psalm 46 legend tends to support a small-c conservative attitude to the past and the values of the present, though (as I said) this does not mean that everyone who finds it persuasive or attractive holds those beliefs.

There is also an element of mild conspiracy in the legend which may add to its appeal. It offers the listener an insight into something which was deliberately hidden from most people, allowing them to be part of an inner circle with special knowledge. This perhaps partly explains its attraction for Baconian groups in the 19th century, who argued that Bacon, rather than Shakespeare, was the author of the works attributed to the latter. Despite the legend showing how Shakespeare's name could be found in the psalm, rather than Bacon's, the element of conspiracy and secret codes seems to have appealed to those who were already committed to a conspiracist view of this period of literary history. This vision of the past, in which the dominant historical narrative is not only wrong, but the result of a deliberate plot to trick everyone, encourages the division of the world into those who are aware of the deception and those who are not. Some believers in the theory that Shakespeare is not the author of Shakespeare's works have even gone so far as declaring that scholars have deliberately ignored or covered up evidence against the playwright, perpetrating an ongoing fraud on the public for their own supposed benefit.

This is hardly the case for the Psalm 46 legend, since no-one (except the Baconians) has suggested that the connection between Shakespeare and the King James Bible is evidence of a grand political or literary deception. It does, however, have certain elements in common with other conspiracist views of Shakespeare and the past: a secret code, a fact hidden from most people, collaboration between powerful figures. When the secret is revealed, however, the outcome is to confirm, rather than question, the legitimacy of the literary and religious establishment in Britain and the US. In this way the legend continues to fit into the small-c conservative approach to the world I mentioned above. It does not undermine the high value placed on Shakespeare or the Bible by many people. It does not suggest that they were forged, or lacking in some way, or subject to improper influence during their compilation. A study of the history of their production is more likely to do that. On the contrary, the conspiratorial element of this story offers a reassuring message, proposing to tell a secret which bolsters the legitimacy of traditional cultural value. It would have been "radical" and subversive to established power in some sense to hide Shakespeare's name in the Biblical text during the 17th century. It is not subversive to claim to have found it there in the 21st century. Indeed part of the attraction of the Psalm 46 legend may be its vindication of a traditional canon and vision of cultural value in a period when many people feel these are under threat, as evidenced, for example, by Alan Bloom's book *The Closing of the American Mind*, or the argument over the proposed removal of the King James Bible from the BBC radio show *Desert Island Discs*. It has some of the hallmarks of a secret, subversive interpretation of history, but with an outcome which confirms a relatively traditional view of cultural values.

This sense that the texts may contain a secret code, and that they will reveal connections to each other, encourages a certain mode of reading which also supports a traditional approach. The legend's plausibility depends on close attention to the words of the texts themselves: it is from the verbal details of the psalm that the figure of Shakespeare appears. An emphasis on the specific words of the text in their specific order is characteristic of the style of literary criticism known as New Criticism, practised most famously by scholars such as I.A. Richards and Cleanth Brooks, and which became dominant in much of school and university English literature teaching during the early 20th century. Its practical methods, which involve a sustained attention to the text's meanings as they are demonstrated by word choice, grammar, syntax and form, are sometimes referred to broadly as "close reading". This contrasted with the often impressionistic and biographical literary criticism carried out in the 19th century, and also with the later 20th century's critical interest in lenses like race, gender and class. To those who champion the kind of close reading which New Criticism made popular, the careful and rigorous attention given to the details of the words and their order involves taking the literary work seriously as a piece of art. It emphasises the value which is inherent in the text itself, and will always be present, since it depends on the formal and technical properties which do not change across time. From this point of view, when Milton (for example) wrote a sonnet, he constructed a verbal work of art which has an internal logic and coherence which continues to exist today.

In contrast, analysing literature from the point of view of class, gender and race would feel to a traditionalist as if the answers were being sought outside the text. Such traditionalist critics, who might be represented today by Harold Bloom, would allege that the critical lenses of race, class and gender are too often attempts to "catch out" the author, to discredit the literary work, and to hold it to account by modern social and ethical standards. The practice of close reading is thus often associated with a canonically-focused attitude to literature and history, which would see itself as reading the works on their own terms, exploring their inherent value and respecting the inheritance of the past.

A somewhat similar contrast can be seen in modern reading of the Bible between an approach which emphasises the Bible as a whole and coherent text which contains everything necessary to understand it, and a more sceptical and critical sensibility which seeks to explore the textual history of the books, the conditions of their production, and the historical forces which shaped the text as we possess it. The former approach is usually associated with a more theologically conservative agenda, which stresses its respect for the Bible, its humility before the text as the revelation of God and the harmony of the Biblical material when read on its own terms. The latter is sometimes criticised as seeking to pick apart the text, thus obscuring its spiritual and moral demands on people in the present, and arrogantly elevating modern scholarly techniques over the wisdom contained within the Bible.

The Biblical scholar Brevard Childs summed up this critique when he suggested that modern scholarship was eager to reduce the Bible to "inert shards". (These are, of course, rather caricatured sketches. There are many theologically conservative people who are deeply engaged with critical scholarship of the Bible, and many critical scholars who place a high value on the intricacy and spiritual meaning of the text. This is how the two emphases are often portrayed, however.) The mode of reading which the Psalm 46 legend depends upon is a close scrutiny of the text in its specific details, and the discerning of a connection to another significant text within it. It thus has something in common with the approaches to both literature and the Bible which sit comfortably within a more conservative view of the world, especially at the beginning of the 21st century.

The legend potentially also satisfies another impulse in reading Shakespeare and the King James Bible: it personalises the story of two great and complex collections of texts, which have had enormous influence on later people's religious and literary lives. There is something instinctively unsatisfactory about the facts that Shakespeare's works are a large corpus of plays and poems which were not all composed in an orderly way for us by the author, and printed directly from manuscripts bearing his handwriting. The irregular and commercial business of playbooks being printed by theatre companies was responsible for the quartos during his life, and a memorial (and also commercial) project by two of his associates after his death gave us the First Folio. The disagreements over which plays contain material by other playwrights, and where in the texts that material might be, continue amongst scholars. The intricacies of textual scholarship break down the works into tiny units, looking at lines and fragments of lines, and subject them to minute analysis. All this scholarship is very worthwhile, and its results can have enormous and radical effects on our understanding of Shakespeare's work and times, but it often lacks the strong personal narrative many people find compelling in history. The "hand" of Shakespeare can feel very far away from the texts as we possess them today. The same might be said of the Bible in English, especially the King James Bible. The historical account, as we have it, is a story of political disagreements, of wrangling over individual words, of committees reviewing, consulting the terms of reference for their project, and appreciating the force of precedent. That story has been fascinatingly told by Adam Nicolson and Benson Bowbrick, amongst others, but it can lack something of the same personal quality that many people look for in the story of Shakespeare. If there is a temptation to ask gloomily where the hand of Shakespeare is in the story of the *Complete Works*, there is a similar temptation to despair of finding a significant hand in the story of the King James Bible. Where is King James' hand? Where, even, is God's? I suspect the Psalm 46 legend satisfies some of this desire for the immediate and the personal in these influential texts.

These seem to me the most likely explanations for the popularity of the legend, and its reappearance in different guises across the 20th century. (Explanations are needed because I think the story is not true and is not supported by any evidence; much less thought would need to be given to why people believed a particular historical fact.)

As I have stressed, these suggestions are not a psychological or political map of people who believe in the legend, nor of those who find it compelling, attractive or interesting. I am not suggesting that belief that Shakespeare's name was hidden (by him or others) in the 46th psalm is a clue to voting record, social background or religious affiliation. I would, however, argue that the legend fits more easily within certain cultural attitudes than others, given the history of Shakespeare and the Bible over the last century or so. Indeed I suspect that the legend's popularity (on a general rather than individual scale) is an expression of more traditional attitudes to the canon and to cultural values, and bound up with a sense that these values are under threat in the modern world. As a story, and as a textual trick, it satisfies impulses and desires around the authority of the religious and literary canon, the correct way to read that canon, and the continuity of current values with those of the past. It suggests, however vaguely, that Shakespeare and the Bible belong together and should be read on their own terms rather than being picked apart or contextualised.

These are texts which have been enormously influential over the past 400 years, and which continue to be valued and read today by millions of people. It is worth noting that they are read in different ways from the majority of other books, and not only in terms of the respect they are accorded. Shakespeare and the Bible are both regularly performed, whether on Broadway productions and end-of-term school plays or in liturgies and Bible readings in church. A large number of people have the experience of not only reading these texts, but reciting them, speaking their lines as if they are their own words, and placing themselves in the role of the figures within the books. Novels, TV shows and lyric poems frequently encourage a strong level of identification between the reader and the characters, but performing Shakespeare requires a kind of inhabiting of the text which takes this a stage further. (Cosplay and other elements of fan culture might be regarded as providing this kind of "immersion" in the text, in another mode.)

The Bible is not (usually) printed in the form of a script, but the services of most Christian denominations involve the public reading of the Scriptures, which are often highly dramatic and involve reported speeches. In the Prophets and the Epistles particularly there are many passages which repeatedly use the second person singular and plural, "you", as if the text is directly addressing those listening. In the more traditional and liturgical services of denominations such as the Roman Catholic and Anglican/Episcopalian churches, much of the liturgy involves the ministers and congregations speaking and responding to each other using Biblical texts, as if these words are their own. (Obviously it will vary as to which version of the Bible is used so these are often not the words of the King James Bible.) The institutions which study and revere these texts encourage a level of participation in them, a kind of inhabiting of the text, which is unusual in its intensity and widespread nature. In this kind of engagement with Shakespeare and the Bible the historical and critical analysis I have been carrying out in this book is likely to seem deeply unimportant, at least in the moment of performance. When I attend a Shakespeare play or take part in a church service, I am not usually running over the textual history of the passages being recited in my head. If I were doing so, I would suspect that something had gone wrong with either me or the performance/service. Thus it is hardly surprising that the issues of textual and production history might be swept aside for some people when a story like the Psalm 46 legend is repeated. It is not illegitimate to engage with these texts in ways other than the historical and analytical: quite the contrary.

Nonetheless, as I have argued throughout this book, the Psalm 46 legend fails to do justice both to the texts of Shakespeare and the King James Bible, and to the astonishing histories of which they are a part. The political, social, religious and literary worlds which gather around these books are far more puzzling, dramatic and absorbing than this little conspiracy theory claims. It claims to tell a secret, but points us away from the heart of the mystery.

Appendix: "Proofs of Holy Writ"

by Rudyard Kipling
(April 1934)

1. Arise, shine: for thy light is come, and the glory of the Lord is risen upon thee.
2. For, behold, the darkness shall cover the earth, and gross darkness the people: but the Lord shall arise upon thee, and his glory shall be seen upon thee.
3. And the Gentiles shall come to thy light, and kings to the brightness of thy rising.
...
19. The sun shall be no more thy light by day; neither for brightness shall the moon give light unto thee: but the Lord shall be unto thee an everlasting light, and thy God thy glory.
20. Thy sun shall no more go down; neither shall thy moon withdraw itself: for the Lord shall be thine everlasting light, and the days of thy mourning shall be ended.

Isaiah 60 (Authorised Version – 1611)

They seated themselves in the heavy chairs on the pebbled floor beneath the eaves of the summer-house by the orchard. A table between them carried wine and glasses, and a packet of papers, with pen and ink. The larger man of the two, his doublet unbuttoned, his broad face blotched and scarred, puffed a little as he came to rest. The other picked an apple from the grass, bit it, and went on with the thread of the talk that they must have carried out of doors with them.

'But why waste time fighting atomies who do not come up to your belly-button, Ben?' he asked.

'It breathes me – it breathes me, between bouts! You'd be better for a tussle or two.'

'But not to spend mind and verse on 'em. What was Dekker to you? Ye knew he'd strike back – and hard.'

'He and Marston had been baiting me like dogs ... about my trade as they called it, though it was only my cursed stepfather's. "Bricks and mortar," Dekker said, and "hodman". And he mocked my face. 'Twas clean as curds in my youth. This humour has come on me since.'

'Ah! "Every man and his humour"? But why did ye not have at Dekker in peace – over the sack, as you do at me?'

'Because I'd have drawn on him – and he's no more worth a hanging than Gabriel. Setting aside what he wrote of me, too, the hireling dog has merit, of a sort. His Shoe-maker's Holiday. Hey? Though my Bartlemy Fair, when 'tis presented, will furnish out three of it and—'

'Ride all the easier. I have suffered two readings of it already. It creaks like an overloaded hay-wain,' the other cut in. 'You give too much.'

Ben smiled loftily, and went on. 'But I'm glad I lashed him in my Poetaster, for all I've worked with him since. How comes it that I've never fought with thee, Will?'

'First, Behemoth', the other drawled, 'it needs two to engender any sort of iniquity. Second, the betterment of this present age—and the next, maybe—lies, in chief, on our four shoulders. If the Pillars of the Temple fall out, Nature, Art, and Learning come to a stand. Last, I am not yet ass enough to hawk up my private spites before the groundlings. What do the Court, citizens, or 'prentices give for thy fallings-out or fallings-in with Dekker – or the Grand Devil?'

'They should be taught, then – taught.'

'Always that? What's your commission to enlighten us?'

'My own learning which I have heaped up, lifelong, at my own pains. My assured knowledge, also, of my craft and art. I'll suffer no man's mock or malice on it.'

'The one sure road to mockery.'

'I deny nothing of my brain-store to my lines. I – I build up my own works throughout.'

'Yet when Dekker cries "hodman" y'are not content.'

Ben half heaved in his chair. 'I'll owe you a beating for that when I'm thinner. Meantime here's on account. I say I build upon my own foundations; devising and perfecting my own plots; adorning 'em justly as fits time, place, and action. In all of which you sin damnably. I set no landward principalities on sea-beaches.'

'They pay their penny for pleasure — not learning,' Will answered above the apple-core.

'Penny or tester, you owe 'em justice. In the facture of plays—nay, listen, Will—at all points they must he dressed historically—*teres atque rotundus*—in ornament and temper. As my Sejanus, of which the mob was unworthy.'

Here Will made a doleful face, and echoed, 'Unworthy! I was – what did I play, Ben, in that long weariness? Some most grievous ass.'

'The part of Caius Silius,' said Ben stiffly.

Will laughed aloud. 'True. "Indeed that place was not my sphere."'

It must have been a quotation, for Ben winced a little, ere he recovered himself and went on: 'Also my Alchemist which the world in part apprehends. The main of its learning is necessarily yet hid from 'em. To come to your works, Will—'

'I am a sinner on all sides. The drink's at your elbow.'

'Confession shall not save ye – nor bribery.' Ben filled his glass. 'Sooner than labour the right cold heat to devise your own plots you filch, botch, and clap 'em together out o' ballads, broadsheets, old wives' tales, chap-books—'

Will nodded with complete satisfaction. 'Say on', quoth he.

'Tis so with nigh all yours. I've known honester jackdaws. And whom among the learned do ye deceive? Reckoning up those—forty, is it?—your plays you've misbegot, there's not six which have not plots common as Moorditch.'

'Ye're out, Ben. There's not one. My *Love's Labour* (how I came to write it, I know not) is nearest to lawful issue. My *Tempest* (how I came to write that, I know) is, in some part my own stuff. Of the rest, I stand guilty. Bastards all!'

'And no shame?'

'None! Our business must be fitted with parts hot and hot – and the boys are more trouble than the men. Give me the bones of any stuff, I'll cover 'em as quickly as any. But to hatch new plots is to waste God's unreturning time like a—' he chuckled, 'like a hen.'

'Yet see what ye miss! Invention next to Knowledge, whence it proceeds, being the chief glory of Art—'

'Miss, say you? Dick Burbage – in my Hamlet that I botched for him when he had staled of our Kings? (Nobly he played it.) Was he a miss?'

Ere Ben could speak Will overbore him.

'And when poor Dick was at odds with the world in general and womankind in special, I clapped him up my *Lear* for a vomit.'

'An hotchpotch of passion, outrunning reason,' was the verdict.

'Not altogether. Cast in a mould too large for any boards to bear. (My fault!) Yet Dick evened it. And when he'd come out of his whoremongering aftermaths of repentance, I served him my Macbeth to toughen him. Was that a miss?'

'I grant your Macbeth as nearest in spirit to my Sejanus; showing for example: "How fortune plies her sports when she begins To practise 'em." We'll see which of the two lives longest.'

'Amen! I'll bear no malice among the worms.'

A liveried man, booted and spurred, led a saddle-horse through a gate into the orchard. At a sign from Will he tethered the beast to a tree, lurched aside, and stretched on the grass. Ben, curious as a lizard, for all his bulk, wanted to know what it meant.

'There's a nosing Justice of the Peace lost in thee,' Will returned. 'Yon's a business I've neglected all this day for thy fat sake – and he by so much the drunker ... Patience! It's all set out on the table. Have a care with the ink!'

Ben reached unsteadily for the packet of papers and read the superscription:

'"To William Shakespeare, Gentleman, at his house of New Place in the town of Stratford, these – with diligence from M.S." Why does the fellow withhold his name? Or is it one of your women? I'll look.'

Muzzy as he was, he opened and unfolded a mass of printed papers expertly enough.

'From the most learned divine, Miles Smith of Brazen Nose College,' Will explained. 'You know this business as well as I. The King has set all the scholars of England to make one Bible, which the Church shall be bound to, out of all the Bibles that men use.'

'I knew.' Ben could not lift his eyes from the printed page. 'I'm more about Court than you think. The learning of Oxford and Cambridge—"most noble and most equal," as I have said—and Westminster, to sit upon a clutch of Bibles. Those 'ud be Geneva (my mother read to me out of it at her knee), Douai, Rheims, Coverdale, Matthew's, the Bishops', the Great, and so forth.'

'They are all set down on the page there – text against text. And you call me a botcher of old clothes?'

'Justly. But what's your concern with this botchery? To keep peace among the Divines? There's fifty of 'em at it as I've heard.'

'I deal with but one. He came to know me when we played at Oxford – when the plague was too hot in London.'

'I remember this Miles Smith now. Son of a butcher? Hey?' Ben grunted.

'Is it so?' was the quiet answer. 'He was moved, he said, with some lines of mine in Dick's part. He said they were, to his godly apprehension, a parable, as it might be, of his reverend self, going down darkling to his tomb 'twixt cliffs of ice and iron.'

'What lines? I know none of thine of that power. But in my Sejanus—'

'"These were in my Macbeth. They lost nothing at Dick's mouth:

> '"To-morrow, and tomorrow, and to-morrow
> Creeps in this petty pace from day to day
> To the last syllable of recorded time,
> And all our yesterdays have lighted fools
> The way to dusty death—"'

or something in that sort. Condell writes 'em out fair for him, and tells him I am Justice of the Peace (wherein he lied) and armiger, which brings me within the pale of God's creatures and the Church. Little and little, then, this very reverend Miles Smith opens his mind to me. He and a half-score others, his cloth, are cast to furbish up the Prophets – Isaiah to Malachi. In his opinion by what he'd heard, I had some skill in words, and he'd condescend—'

'How?' Ben barked. 'Condescend?'

'Why not? He'd condescend to inquire o' me privily, when direct illumination lacked, for a tricking-out of his words or the turn of some figure. For example,' Will pointed to the papers, 'here be the first three verses of the Sixtieth of Isaiah, and the nineteenth and twentieth of that same. Miles has been at a stand over 'em a week or more.'

'They never called on me.' Ben caressed lovingly the hand-pressed proofs on their lavish linen paper. 'Here's the Latin atop and'—his thick forefinger ran down the slip—'some three – four – Englishings out of the other

Bibles. They spare 'emselves nothing. Let's to it together. Will you have the Latin first?'

'Could I choke ye from that, Holofernes?'

Ben rolled forth, richly: '"Surge, illumare, Jerusalem, quia venit lumen tuum, et gloria Domini super te orta est. Quia ecce tenebrae aperient terram et caligo populos. Super te autem orietur Dominus, et gloria ejus in te videbitur. Et ambulabunt gentes in lumine tuo, et reges in splendore ortus tui." Er-hum? Think you to better that?'

'How have Smith's crew gone about it?'

'Thus.' Ben read from the paper. '"Get thee up, O Jerusalem, and be bright, for thy light is at hand. and the glory of God has risen up upon thee."'

'Up-pup-up!' Will stuttered profanely.

Ben held on. '"See how darkness is upon the earth and the peoples thereof."'

'That's no great stuff to put into Isaiah's mouth. And further, Ben?'

"'But on thee God shall shew light and on—" or "in," is it?' (Ben held the proof closer to the deep furrow at the bridge of his nose.) "'On thee shall His glory be manifest. So that all peoples shall walk in thy light and the Kings in the glory of thy morning.'"

'It may be mended. Read me the Coverdale of it now. 'Tis on the same sheet – to the right, Ben.'

'Umm-umm! Coverdale saith, "And therefore get thee up betimes, for thy light cometh, and the glory of the Lord shall rise up upon thee. For lo! while the darkness and cloud covereth the earth and the people, the Lord shall shew thee light, and His glory shall be seen in thee. The Gentiles shall come to thy light, and kings to the brightness that springeth forth upon thee." But "gentes" is for the most part, "peoples"' Ben concluded.

'Eh?' said Will indifferently. 'Art sure?'

This loosed an avalanche of instances from Ovid, Quintilian, Terence, Columella, Seneca, and others. Will took no heed till the rush ceased. but stared into the orchard through the September haze. 'Now give me the

Douai and Geneva for this "Get thee up, O Jerusalem,"' said he at last.

'They'll be all there.' Ben referred to the proofs. ''Tis "arise" in both,' said he. '"Arise and be bright" in Geneva. In the Douai 'tis "Arise and be illuminated."'

'So? Give me the paper now.' Will took it from his companion, rose, and paced towards a tree in the orchard, turning again, when he had reached it, by a well-worn track through the grass. Ben leaned forward in his chair. The other's free hand went up warningly. 'Quiet, man!' said he. 'I wait on my Demon!' He fell into the stage-stride of his art at that time, speaking to the air.

'How shall this open? "Arise?" No! "Rise!" Yes. And we'll no weak coupling. 'Tis a call to a City! "Rise – shine" ... Nor yet any schoolmaster's "because" – because Isaiah is not Holofernes. "Rise – shine; for thy light is come, and—!"' He refreshed himself from the apple and the proofs as he strode. '"And – and the glory of God!" – No "God"'s over short. We need the long roll here.'

"'And the glory of the Lord is risen on thee." (Isaiah speaks the part. We'll have it from his own lips.) What's next in Smith's stuff? ... "See how?" Oh, vile – vile! ... And Geneva hath "Lo"? (Still, Ben! Still!) "Lo" is better by all odds: but to match the long roll of "the Lord" we'll have it "Behold". How goes it now? For, behold, darkness clokes the earth and – and – What's the colour and use of this cursed caligo, Ben? – "Et caligo populos."'

'"Mistiness" or, as in Pliny, "blindness". And further—'

'No-o ... Maybe, though, caligo will piece out tenebrae. "Quia ecce tenebrae operient terram et caligo populos." Nay! "Shadow" and "mist" are not men enough for this work ... Blindness. did ye say, Ben? ... The blackness of "blindness" atop of mere darkness? ... By God, I've used it in my own stuff many times! "Gross" searches it to the hilts! "Darkness covers" – no – "clokes" (short always). "Darkness clokes the earth, and gross – gross darkness the people!" (But Isaiah's prophesying, with the storm behind him. Can ye not feel it, Ben? It must be "shall") – "Shall cloke the earth" ... The rest comes clearer .... But on thee God Shall arise" ... (Nay, that's sacrificing the Creator to the Creature!) "But the Lord shall arise on thee", and—yes, we sound that "thee" again—"and on thee shall" – No! ... "And His glory shall be seen on thee." Good!' He walked his beat a little in silence, mumbling the two verses before he mouthed them.

'I have it! Heark, Ben! "Rise – shine; for thy light is come, and the glory of the Lord is risen on thee. For, behold, darkness shall cloke the earth, and gross darkness the people. But the Lord shall arise on thee, and His glory shall be seen upon thee."'

'There's something not all amiss there,' Ben conceded.

'My Demon never betrayed me yet, while I trusted him. Now for the verse that runs to the blast of rams'-horns. "Et ambulabunt gentes in lumine tuo, et reges in splendore ortus tui." How goes that in the Smithy? "The Gentiles shall come to thy light, and kings to the brightness that springs forth upon thee?" The same in Coverdale and the Bishops' – eh? We'll keep "Gentiles", Ben, for the sake of the indraught of the last syllable. But it might be "And the Gentiles shall draw." No! The plainer the better! "The Gentiles shall come to thy light, and kings to the splendour of—" (Smith's out here! We'll need something that shall lift the trumpet anew.) "Kings shall – shall – Kings to –" (Listen, Ben, but on your life speak not!) "Gentiles shall come to thy light, and kings to thy bright-ness" – No! "Kings to the brightness that springeth—" Serves not! ... One trumpet must answer another. And the blast of a trumpet is always ai-ai. "The brightness of" – "Ortus" signifies "rising", Ben – or what?'

'Ay, or "birth", or the East in general.'

'Ass! 'Tis the one word that answers to "light". "Kings to the brightness of thy rising." Look! The thing shines now within and without. God! That so much should lie on a word!' He repeated the verse – "And the Gentiles shall come to thy light, and kings to the brightness of thy rising."'

He walked to the table and wrote rapidly on the proof margin all three verses as he had spoken them. 'If they hold by this', said he, raising his head, 'they'll not go far astray. Now for the nineteenth and twentieth verses.

On the other sheet, Ben. What? What? Smith says he has held back his rendering till he hath seen mine? Then we'll botch 'em as they stand. Read me first the Latin; next the Coverdale, and last the Bishops'. There's a contagion of sleep in the air.' He handed back the proofs, yawned, and took up his walk.

Obedient, Ben began: '"Non erit tibi amplius Sol ad lucendum per diem, nec splendor Lunae illuminabit te." Which Coverdale rendereth, "The Sun shall never be thy day light, and the light of the Moon shall never shine unto thee." The Bishops read: "Thy sun shall never be thy daylight and the light of the moon shall never shine on thee."'

'Coverdale is the better,' said Will, and, wrinkling his nose a little, 'The Bishops put out their lights clumsily. Have at it, Ben.'

Ben pursed his lips and knit his brow. 'The two verses are in the same mode, changing a hand's-breadth in the second. By so much, therefore, the more difficult.'

'Ye see that, then?' said the other, staring past him, and muttering as he paced, concerning suns and moons.

Presently he took back the proof, chose him another apple, and grunted. 'Umm-umm! "Thy Sun shall never be – No! Flat as a split viol. "Non erit tibi amplius Sol—" That amplius must give tongue.

Ah! . . . "Thy Sun shall not – shall not – shall no more be thy light by day" A fair entry. "Nor?" – No! Not on the heels of "day". "Neither" it must be – "Neither the Moon" – but here's splendor and the rams'-horns again. (Therefore – ai-ai!) "Neither for brightness shall the Moon—" (Pest! It is the Lord who is taking the Moon's place over Israel. It must be "thy Moon".) "Neither for brightness shall thy Moon light – give – make – give light unto thee." Ah! ... Listen here! ... "The Sun shall no more be thy light by day: neither for brightness shall thy Moon give light unto thee." That serves, and more, for the first entry. What next, Ben?'

Ben nodded magisterially as Will neared him, reached out his hand for the proofs, and read: '"Sed erit tibi Dominus in lucem sempiternam et Deus tuus in gloriam tuam." Here is a jewel of Coverdale's that the Bishops have wisely stolen whole. Hear! "But the Lord Himself shall be thy everlasting light, and thy God shall be thy glory."' Ben paused. 'There's a hand's-breadth of splendour for a simple man to gather!'

'Both hands rather. He's swept the strings as divinely as David before Saul', Will assented. 'We'll convey it whole, too... What's amiss now, Holofernes?'

For Ben was regarding him with a scholar's cold pity. 'Both hands! Will, hast thou ever troubled to master any shape or sort of prosody — the mere names of the measures and pulses of strung words?'

'I beget some such stuff and send it to you to christen. What's your wisdomhood in labour of?'

'Naught. Naught. But not to know the names of the tools of his trade!' Ben half muttered and pronounced some Greek word or other which conveyed nothing to the listener, who replied: 'Pardon, then, for whatever sin it was. I do but know words for my need of 'em. Ben. Hold still awhile!'

He went back to his pacings and mutterings. '"For the Lord Himself shall be thy — or thine? — everlasting light." Yes. We'll convey that.' He repeated it twice.

'Nay! Can be bettered. Hark ye, Ben. Here is the Sun going up to over-run and possess all Heaven for evermore. Therefore (Still, man!) we'll harness the horses of the dawn. Hear their hooves? "The Lord Himself shall be unto thee thy everlasting light, and—" Hold again! After that climbing thunder must be some smooth check – like great wings gliding. Therefore we'll not have "shall be thy glory," but "And thy God thy glory!" Ay – even as an eagle alighteth! Good – good! Now again, the sun and moon of that twentieth verse, Ben.'

Ben read: '"Non occidet ultra Sol tuus et Luna tua non minuetur: quia erit tibi Dominus in lucem sempiternam et complebuntur dies luctus tui."'

Will snatched the paper and read aloud from the Coverdale version. '"Thy Sun shall never go down, and thy Moon shall not be taken away ..." What a plague's Coverdale doing with his blocking ets and urs, Ben? What's minuetur? ... I'll have it all anon.'

'Minish – make less – appease – abate, as in—'

'So?' Will threw the proofs back. 'Then "wane" should serve. "Neither shall thy moon wane ... "Wane" is good, but over-weak for place next to "moon"' ... He swore softly. 'Isaiah hath abolished both earthly sun and moon. Exeunt ambo. Aha! I begin to see! ... Sol, the man, goes down—down stairs or trap—as needs be. Therefore "Go down" shall stand. "Set" would have been better—as a sword sent home in the scabbard— but it jars – it jars. Now Luna must retire herself in some simple fashion ... Which? Ass that I be! 'Tis common talk in all the plays ...'

"Withdrawn"..."Favour withdrawn"..."Countenance withdrawn." "The Queen withdraws herself"... "Withdraw," it shall be! "Neither shall thy moon withdraw herself." (Hear her silver train rasp the boards, Ben?) "Thy sun shall no more go down – neither shall thy moon withdraw herself. For the Lord..."—ay, the Lord, simple of Himself—"shall be thine"—yes, "thine" here—"everlasting light, and" ... How goes the ending, Ben?'

"'Et complebuntur dies luctus tui.'" Ben read. "'And thy sorrowful days shall be rewarded thee," says Coverdale.'

'And the Bishops?'

'"And thy sorrowful days shall be ended."'

'By no means. And Douai?'

'"Thy sorrow shall be ended."'

'And Geneva?'

'"And the days of thy mourning shall be ended."'

'The Switzers have it! Lay the tail of Geneva to the head of Coverdale and the last is without flaw.'

He began to thump Ben on the shoulder. 'We have it! I have it all, Boanerges! Blessed be my Demon! Hear!

'"The sun shall no more be thy light by day, neither for brightness the moon by night. But the Lord Himself shall be unto thee thy everlasting light, and thy God thy glory."'

He drew a deep breath and went on.

'"Thy sun shall no more go down; neither shall thy moon withdraw herself, for the Lord shall be thine everlasting light, and the days of thy mourning shall be ended.'"

The rain of triumphant blows began again. 'If those other seven devils in London let it stand on this sort, it serves. But God knows what they can not turn upsee-dejee!'

Ben wriggled. 'Let be!' he protested. 'Ye are more moved by this jugglery than if the Globe were burned.'

'Thatch – old thatch! And full of fleas! ... But, Ben, ye should have heard my Ezekiel making mock of fallen Tyrus in his twenty-seventh chapter. Miles sent me the whole, for, he said, some small touches. I took it to the Bank – four o'clock of a summer morn; stretched out in one of our wherries – and watched London, Port and Town, up and down the river, waking all arrayed to heap more upon evident excess. Ay! "A merchant for the peoples of many isles" ... "The ships of Tarshish did sing of thee in thy markets"? Yes! I saw all Tyre before me neighing her pride against lifted heaven ... But what will they let stand of all mine at long last? Which? I'll never know.'

He had set himself neatly and quickly to refolding and cording the packet while he talked. 'That's secret enough,' he said at the finish.

'He'll lose it by the way.' Ben pointed to the sleeper beneath the tree. 'He's owl-drunk.'

'But not his horse,' said Will. He crossed the orchard, roused the man; slid the packet into an holster which he carefully rebuckled; saw him out of the gate, and returned to his chair.

'Who will know we had part in it?' Ben asked.

'God, maybe – if He ever lay ear to earth. I've gained and lost enough – lost enough.' He lay back and sighed. There was long silence till he spoke half aloud. 'And Kit that was my master in the beginning, he died when all the world was young.'

'Knifed on a tavern reckoning – not even for a wench!' Ben nodded.

'Ay. But if he'd lived he'd have breathed me! 'Fore God, he'd have breathed me!'

'Was Marlowe, or any man, ever thy master, Will?'

'He alone. Very he. I envied Kit. Ye do not know that envy, Ben?'

'Not as touching my own works. When the mob is led to prefer a baser Muse, I have felt the hurt, and paid home. Ye know that – as ye know my doctrine of play-writing.'

'Nay—not wholly—tell it at large,' said Will, relaxing in his seat, for virtue had gone out of him. He put a few drowsy questions. In three minutes Ben had launched full-flood on the decayed state of the drama, which he was born to correct; on cabals and intrigues against him which he had fought without cease; and on the inveterate muddle-headedness of the mob unless duly scourged into approbation by his magisterial hand.

It was very still in the orchard now that the horse had gone. The heat of the day held though the sun sloped and the wine had done its work. Presently, Ben's discourse was broken by a snort from the other chair.

'I was listening, Ben! Missed not a word – missed not a

word.' Will sat up and rubbed his eyes. 'Ye held me throughout.' His head dropped again before he had done speaking.

Ben looked at him with a chuckle and quoted from one of his own plays:

"'Mine earnest vehement botcher And deacon also, Will, I cannot dispute with you.'"

He drew out flint, steel and tinder, pipe and tobacco-bag from somewhere round his waist, lit and puffed against the midges till he, too, dozed.

Further Reading

Shakespeare and the Bible are two of the largest scholarly fields in the arts and humanities, and it would be impossible to provide a reading list which covers their major points. However, the following books might be of interest to anyone wishing to follow up on some of the directions in which the present book has pointed.

Jem Bloomfield, *Words of Power: Reading Shakespeare and the Bible*

Benson Bowbrick, *The Making of the English Bible*

Susan Gillingham, *The Poems and Psalms of the Hebrew Bible*

Beatrice Groves, *Texts and Traditions*

Hannibal Hamlin, *The Bible in Shakespeare; Psalm Culture and Early Modern English Literature*

Adam Nicolson, *Power and Glory*

David Norton, *A History of the English Bible as Literature*

Emma Smith, *The Cambridge Introduction to Shakespeare; The Making of Shakespeare's First Folio*

Naomi Tadmor, *The Social Universe of the English Bible*

Gary Taylor, *Reinventing Shakespeare*

Endnotes

[1] Mike Savage et al., *Social Class in the 21st Century*, (London: Penguin 2014), p. 90. Indeed the association between being a member of the social and economic elite and attending the theatre regularly was apparently so intuitive to most of the people being surveyed in this study that the researchers noted that demand for tickets at London theatres rose on average by nearly 200% in the week after the survey was launched by the BBC. Simply by asking questions about people's engagement with cultural and artistic life (along with their social experiences, background and economic situation), the researchers had affected the patterns of that engagement by making people more conscious of what they already knew about how social and economic class in Britain works. Tellingly, their reaction to this conscious awareness was to seek out theatre tickets: to behave in a way that they knew would mark them as part of the social elite. (Savage, p. 6.)

[2] They may not have been wrong, of course, that theatres were part of the plague problem: packing thousands of unwashed and unwell people into a small space for hours at a time is a fairly good way to ensure that whatever infectious diseases any of them have are given the best chance of incubation and transmission. But the Puritans had a rather more direct and dramatic notion of God's judgement than the efficient spread of microbes due to poor health and safety regulations in entertainment venues.

[3] The instructions are given here in the modernised spelling version provided by Gordon Campbell; they can be found, with an excellent commentary on each, in Campbell's *Bible: The Story of the King James Bible 1611–2011* (Oxford: Oxford University Press, 2010) and another set of comments is provided by Adam Nicolson's *Power and Glory: Jacobean England and the Making of the King James Bible* (US edition title: *God's Secretaries*, reissued in 2011 as *When God Spoke English*).

[4] "John Rainolds", *Oxford Dictionary of National Biography*

[5] "Laurence Chaderton", *Oxford Dictionary of National Biography*.

[6] Baxter's book appeared significantly later in the 17th century, but provides a good example of the attitudes towards theatre which continued through the era. Richard Baxter, *The Reformed Pastor*, ed. Samuel Palmer (London: 1808) p.24

[7] John Jewel, *The Apology of the Church of England*, (Scriptura Press, 2016), n.pag.

[8] It is also a phrase that recalls the title of Shakespeare's play *Much Ado About nothing*, but there really is not space to disappear off on another Shakespeare-based Bible investigation at this moment. Shakespeare was very unlikely to have been involved in the translation of the 1537 Antwerp version, by reason of not yet being born. More seriously, the coincidence of stumbling upon what

seems to be a Shakespearean title in this unconnected text demonstrates the way patterns will appear in any set of texts studied intently enough. As with the Psalm 46 legend, the words "much ado" jump out of this passage not because it is connected to Shakespeare but because Shakespeare is the most important thing about this period to many modern readers. We are so familiar with his words that this occurrence of the phrase might look like a connection.

[9] ll. 4-8, *Beowulf: A Student Edition*, ed. George Jack (Oxford: OUP, 1997), p.24

[10] A description of these features, an account of the scholars who have proposed them, and an application of them to test their reliability, are given in Gillingham's *The Poems and Psalms of the Hebrew Bible*. (Oxford: OUP, 1994)

[11] Ps. 5: 1

[12] Ps. 6:1

[13] Ps. 15:1

[14] Ps. 17:2

[15] Ps. 19:1

[16] quoted in Gillingham, *The Poems and Psalms of the Hebrew Bible*, p.196–7

[17] Brown, *The Oxford Handbook of the Psalms*, p.151

[18] Gillingham, *Poems and Psalms of the Hebrew Bible*, p.197

[19] Paul Edmondson and Stanley Wells, *Shakespeare's Sonnets*, (Oxford; Oxford University Press, 2004), p.44

[20] Those meanings include, according to Edmonson and Wells, the possibility that the young man to whom some of the sonnets are addressed was also called "Will".

[21] Hannibal Hamlin, *Psalm Culture and Early Modern English Literature*, (Cambridge: CUP, 2004).

[22] *The Winter's Tale*, IV. 3. 42–5.

[23] *1 Henry IV*, II. 4. 126–7.

[24] Thomas Sternhold, John Hopkins and others, *The Whole Book of Psalms*, (London: GW, 1635), n.pag.

[25] Mary Sidney and Philip Sidney, *The Sidney Psalter*, (Oxford: OUP, 2009)

[26] Sidney and Sidney, *The Sidney Psalter*.

[27] Gillingham, *Psalms through the Centuries: Vol I* (Oxford: Wiley-Blackwell, 2012), n.pag.

[28] William Clarence Johnson, *Spenser's Amoretti: Analogies of Love* (London and Toronto: Associated University Presses, 1990), p.152

[29] Edmund Spenser, *The Poetical Works of Edmund Spenser*, ed. Charles Cowden Clark, (Edinburgh: William Nimmo, 1868) p.235

[30] As discussed in Randall Martin's article 'Shakespearian Biography, Biblical Allusion and Early Modern Reading Practices', *Shakespeare Survey*, 63, (Cambridge, 2010).

[31] Sidney Lee, *A Life of William Shakespeare*, (London: Smith, Elder and Company, 1908), p.17

[32] Both examples appear in Naseeb Shaheen, *Biblical References in Shakespeare's Plays*, (Newark: University of Delaware Press, 1999), p.34

[33] I am grateful to Prof. Peter McCullough for this example, which fascinated me as an undergraduate student when he used it in a lecture, and sowed one of the seeds of my later interest in Biblical Studies.

[34] *Midsummer Night's Dream*, IV. 1. 185ff.

[35] 1 Corinthians 2:9–10.

[36] I am assuming that however brilliant at listening the audience were in church, they would probably not be able to mentally count the words forwards and backwards at the same time and notice the word positions, whilst the Psalm was being read. Of course it would be possible to argue that the Psalm acrostics were intended

for readers, rather than audiences, and that Shakespeare (or the translators) intended the secret message to only be understood by readers. But Shakespeare wrote the majority of his works for public performance, and when he hid his own name in the more private sonnets, he did so in a way which meant that it could be heard and enjoyed when they were read out.

[37] Hamlin, *The Bible in Shakespeare*, p. 59.

[38] ibid. p.60.

[39] ibid. pp.60–1.

[40] James Shapiro makes this argument startlingly in *Contested Will*.

[41] quoted in Gary Taylor, *Reinventing Shakespeare: A Cultural History from the Restoration to the Present*, (Oxford: OUP, 1989) p. 165.

[42] quoted in Taylor, *Reinventing Shakespeare*, p.166

[43] ibid. p.167.

[44] ibid. p. 167.

[45] ibid..167.

[46] David Norton, *A History of the English Bible as Literature*, (Cambridge, CUP, 2000) p.299

[47] quoted in Norton, *A History of the English Bible as Literature*, p.303.

[48] ibid. p.310.

[49] quoted in Norton, *A History of the English Bible as Literature*, p.311.

[50] Thomas Hughes *Tom Brown's Schooldays* (repr. London: Macmillan, 1870) p.104

[51] ibid. p.40.

[52] ibid. p.134.

[53] ibid. p.182.

[54] *Julius Caesar*, III. 2.73–7

[55] Genesis 16:11–12.

[56] Anthony Trollope, *The Struggles of Brown, Jones and Robinson*, (London: Smith, Elder and Company, 1870) p.5

[57] Anthony Trollope, *Rachel Ray*, (London: Chapman and Hall, 1863) p.204.

[58] Matthew, 9:17.

[59] Anthony Trollope, *The Belton Estate*, (Leipzig: Taughnitz, 1866), p.120

[60] *Othello*, III. 3. 360.

[61] P.G. Wodehouse, *The Gold Bat and other School Stories*, (repr. London: Penguin 1986) p.70

[62] Wodehouse, *The Gold Bat*, p.80.

[63] Wodehouse, *The Gold Bat*, p.19-20.

[64] Genesis 41:1–4.

[65] Exodus 32:3--4.

[66] *Love's Labour's Lost*, III. 1 144–7.

[67] *Othello* III. 3. 331–5.

[68] Rudyard Kipling, *Something of Myself And Other Autobiographical Writings,* ed. Thomas Pinney, (Cambridge: Cambridge University Press, 1990), p.121–2

[69] *Henry VIII, or All Is True,* III. 2. 440–2

[70] John Donne, *The Works of John Donne*, ed. Henry Alford (London: John Parker, 1839), vol III, p.477.

[71] Raymond Chapman, ed. *Before the King's Majesty: The Life and Writings of Lancelot Andrewes*, (Norwich: Canterbury Press, 2008), p.36

[72] T.S. Eliot, *Selected Essays 1917-1932* (New York: Harcourt, Brace and Company, 1932) p. 295.

[73] Rudyard Kipling, *Puck of Pook's Hill*

[74] Ronald Hutton's *The Triumph of the Moon: A History of Modern Pagan Witchcraft* provides a discussion of these trends in thought about folklore and history in the early 20th century, as well as a

rigorous analysis of the incorrect assumptions many of them were based upon.

[75] His attitude might be compared with Matthew Paris and Ian Hislop, both quintessentially "English" figures of a certain age, class and public reputation, whose writing and broadcasting on such characteristically—even caricaturedly—English subject as cricket, railways and English villages is similarly rooted in the fact that both men grew up outside England in the British Empire, and only "returned" to it in later years.

[76] Nancy L. deClaissé-Walford, Rolf A. Jacobson and Beth LaNeel Tanner, *The Book of Psalms (The New International Commentary on the Old Testament)* (Grand Rapids, Michigan: Eeerdmans, 2014) ebook, n.pag.

[77] Robert Johnson, *A Sermon A Day*, Vol. 2, p.61

[78] Nolan Harmon, *Ministerial Ethics and Etiquette* (repr. Nashville: Abingdon Press, 1987), p.116. To these examples could be added a flurry of others which underline the point, and show the formula being used to introduce a variety of narratives: "The story is told of a woman who, after receiving the proofs of her portrait, was angry with the photographer. She stalked back to him and arrived with these angry words: 'This picture does not do me justice!'" (*Show Me How To Illustrate Evangelistic Sermons*, R. Larry Moyer); "When using a story illustration, real integrity can be given to the story by using

an image or phrase from the illustration later on in the sermon. For example: the story is told that when Sherman marched to the sea, a little old lady refused to leave her home in rural Georgia." (*Creative Preaching and Oral Writing*, Richard C. Hoefler); "The story is told of a church that built a sanctuary of stone with the words 'We preach Christ crucified' engraved above the entrance. A generation of preachers stood in the pulpit of that church and proclaimed the crucified Christ. As a result, many sinners came to saving faith in the Lord. But as the years passed, ivy began to creep up the side of the church's walls..." (*Planning Your Preaching*, Stephen Nelson Rummage); "The story is told of a little boy who attended church on the other side of town from where he lived. He passed several churches on the way to his church. Someone asked him why he went so far to church and he replied, 'You know they love a fellow over there.' I wish this could be said concerning our church." (*One of the Whosoevers: A Life Story and a Collection of Sermons*, G.C. Mccutchen, Sr.).

[79] L. Ted Smith, *A Listening Season: Sermons for Advent and Christmas*, (2010) p.32

[80] This is particularly important, given the emphasis laid in much Evangelical thought on the truth and completeness of the Bible. Part of the problem with Catholic practices to many Evangelicals is that they appear to elevate interpretative traditions, legends about

the saints, and other aspects of their faith life, to the status of the Bible. Given the quantity of material in the Bible which has the appearance of a legend with a moral message —the story of Jonah, for example, or the feeding of the 5000—it might be particularly important for preachers to separate the anecdotes and illustrations they use from the Biblical material, in case listeners begin to think of the Bible stories as simply the equivalent of a man going fishing with an unusual dog, or an old lady shaking her broom at Sherman's army.

[81] The earlier part of this story is told in engrossing detail in Michael Dobson's *The Making of the National Poet*, which traces the arc of Shakespeare's development from out-of-date writer to towering cultural icon. Gary Taylor's *Reinventing Shakespeare* offers a brilliant and irreverent account of how each era created the Shakespeare they wanted, and how Shakespeare thus became all things to all people, and eventually saturated English-speaking culture.

[82] In the specific case of Psalm 46, with its declaration that "Therefore will not we fear, though the earth be removed, and though the mountains be carried into the midst of the sea", a modern Christian could even read our increased knowledge of geology and earth's history as increasing the religious meaning of the line. If God is trusted to be stalwart even when such things

happen, and scientists discovered that exactly these things have happened, then the verses might be read as assuring the listener of God's care and power despite the unsettling effect of modern knowledge. However, in the original context of the line itself it is clear that the rhetorical force of imagining God's trustworthiness in these situations (earth moving, mountains tumbling into seas) depends upon an assumption that they have not happened and would be absolutely catastrophic if they ever did.

[83] Yvonne Sherwood and Stephen D. Moore, *The Invention of the Biblical Scholar: A Critical Manifesto* (Minneapolis: Fortress Press, 2011), p.94

[84] Northrop Frye, *The Great Code: The Bible and Literature* (1982, repr.) p.5, 12, 13.

[85] Tom Wright, *Finding God in the Psalms: Sing, Pray, Live* (SPCK: 2014) e-book n.pag.

[86] George W. Knight, *The Bible as a Literary Treasure*, (2010) e-book n.pag.

Made in the USA
Middletown, DE
31 August 2017